1

Incarcerations in Black and White

Have the courage to say no. Have the courage to face the truth. Do the right thing because it is right. These are the magic keys to living with integrity.

~ W. Clement Stone

Also by Christi Griffin

21 Days to Joy: A Daily Devotional to Finding Joy

INCARCERATIONS IN BLACK AND WHITE

The Subjugation of Black America

CHRISTI M. GRIFFIN, JD

INCARCERATIONS IN BLACK AND WHITE

The Subjugation of Black America

By   CHRISTI M. GRIFFIN, JD

Published by: C. Griffin Publishing
PO Box 23422
St. Louis, MO 63156 USA

October, 2013, 50 years after the March on Washington
and 150 years since the Emancipation Proclamation.

ISBN 10   0-9821190-1-1

Printed in the USA

DEDICATION

This book is dedicated to our children. The innocent
victims who suffer the loss of parents to
incarceration. Their pain is the greatest crime of all.

TABLE OF CONTENTS

ACKNOWLEDGEMENTS

This book would not be possible without those who give so much to the ongoing work of The Ethics Project. My unending thanks goes to the active members of the Board of Directors, Chairman, Rev. Dr. Douglass Petty, Atty. Kymberly Smith Jackson, Caroline Fisher, Brittani McClure Williams, St. Louis Health Commissioner Melba Moore, Rev. Douglas Parham, Redditt Hudson, Robin Boyce, Leon Sharpe and Tony Neal. To The Ethics Project's research assistants, Yaa Sarpong, a current law student at Columbia Law School and a gifted CORO Fellow made possible by Rev. Starsky Wilson of The Deaconess Foundation and Haley Levy, a bright student at Washington University in St. Louis. Both provided invaluable research as well as insight from the perspective of a younger generation. To Rev. Rodney Francis and his wife, Dr. Leah Francis Gunning whose eager support and vigorous conversations inspire me to reach new heights. To all those who have served on the Urban League Public Safety Advisory Council, especially St. Louis County Police Captain Doyle, Sgt. Mann, Sgt. Rice and Sgt. Eckhert and many officers with the St. Louis County and St. Louis Metropolitan Police Departments for giving me hope that caring law-enforcement actually exists. To Michael McMillan for your leadership. To retired U.S. Marshall Ron Henderson and Captain John Hayden who headed the St. Louis City Department of Internal Affairs, the first two voices that guided me at the inception of TEP.

To the members of the St. Louis Initiative to Reduce Violence, Rev. B.T. Rice, retired Urban League President James Buford, retired St. Louis Police Chief and current Professor of Criminology Dan Isom, Police Chief Sam Dotson, Police Chief Tim Fitch, Professor Richard Rosenthal, Nancy McCarthy, Evan Krauss, Rosie Stafford, Joe Yancy, Mickey Thomas, and especially Dr. Kelvin Adams, Superintendent of the St. Louis Public Schools, who has kept his door often and provided opportunities, support and challenges. To my hero, Dr. Art McCoy, more than 20 years my junior but a priceless soul I greatly admire. To school superintendents George Henry, Dr. Joylynn Pruitt and Dr. Clive Coleman, To Former Missouri Supreme Court Judge, Ronnie White and Major Rochelle Jones, the St. Louis City Night Chief who has been a stalwart supporter. To Gentry Trotter, for providing a voice to a much needed issue. To Rev. C. Jessel Strong, President of the St. Louis Clergy Coalition and the Coalition itself for having my back. To Adolphus Pruitt, President of the St. Louis Branch of the NAACP and Chair of the Missouri Conference, to Halbert Sullivan founder of The Father Support Center with whom I got off to a rocky start but have found a friend and co-hort. To David Steward, CEO of Worldwide Technology for his constant wisdom and help. To Tom George, Chancellor of the University of Missouri St. Louis, for his constant support. To U.S. Ambassador Andrew Young, for patiently hearing my thoughts and convincing me it is about the economics. I finally believed. To my cousin, Carole Ann Scott and my best friend, Dr. Marilyn Maxwell, both who constantly keep me lifted in prayer. To my "sister" Ilyasah Shabazz for upholding her father's legacy, her mother's hospitality and service and for her incredible strength. To Isabel Wilkerson for encouraging me to keep going. To Joy DeGruy Leary for her work in bringing truth to light and for her willingness to support the NY project. We'll get it done. To all the pastors who opened the doors of their church, especially Rev. Sammie Jones and Rev. Edmund Lowe, who co-hosted the Lunch with Judge Jimmie Edwards. To Judge Edwards, my law school classmate and hero to many. To the principals at Sumner, Roosevelt, Sumner and Vashon high schools in St. Louis who squeezed out time to help guide me in their schools. To Lucius, Brad and the building staff who make being home such a joy. To Victor Woods, an incredibly gifted speaker and staunch ally. And of course, it goes without saying, that I deeply thank my mother, my children and their spouses for their ongoing support, encouragement, patience and love. I love each of you dearly.

Needless to say, I thank God, my Father, who plucked me from among the thickets, brushed me off and gave me the courage and strength to at least try to make a difference in a world with so much to give.

PREFACE

We all have a story. What follows is part of mine. Once blinded by idealism and an unwavering faith in the rule of law, the facts that follow reshaped my very being. I pray they shape yours as well.

Over the last six years I have often been asked why I founded The Ethics Project, a non-profit organization started in 2007, to address the lack of ethics in the criminal justice system that leads to the over arrest, prosecution, conviction, sentencing and incarceration of African Americans and other minorities. Those who asked wondered why I would leave a lucrative law practice to devote my time and energy to the issue of incarcerations. They questioned why I would move out of a plush downtown office with a view of the city and surrender my home surrounded by a lush golf course and manicured lawns. The answer is both simple and complex, I had worked hard to build my practice and as an African American female growing up in the inner city, I had been victimized by nearly every crime on the books. The transition just does not fit.

After 19 years of practicing bankruptcy law, representing nearly 10,000 clients and going above the call of duty for most, then experiencing the most massive change in both law and practice in the history of the U.S. Bankruptcy Code, I was simply burned out. Despite having thought such a day would never come, the years of sitting behind a desk for more hours than you could image, decades of sifting through stacks of files and mounds of pleadings; month after month answering an unending flood of calls and juggling court hearings with children in three different schools, I was simply ready to quit. For several years I had yearned to be creative, to return to the classroom, to teach others the wealth of knowledge accumulated over the years. I was ready to take down my shingle and head for higher ground.

That burnout, however, does not explain the transition. It does not explain why I would go from having far more money than I needed to never having enough; why I would walk away from the power of the law to relying solely on the power of God. It does not explain why I stopped donating to over 30 charities, to being the charity in need.

It does explain, however, why I developed a financial coaching practice that would help my clients better understand their financial behavior, to understand credit practices and to encourage them to excel beyond their current circumstances. That effort allowed me to creatively market myself, (though sudden increased referrals made marketing unnecessary) to teach my clients new skills and to see their immediate transformation. While that practice enjoyed immediate and enormous success, it was short lived. As God has shown me at so many junctures in my life, He had another plan in mind.

With the decision once again, to go above and beyond the call of duty to protect a client against the predatory practice of a neighbor, my eyes were opened to the reality and extent of man's weakness and the extent of the power of sin. What made me close my practice and start a fledgling non-profit organization is a testimony to the power of God. It is a story of David and Goliath, of perseverance, victory and after much anguish and tears, ultimately of joy. This is my story; a woman who practiced law as a ministry for 23 years and saw it destroyed for doing exactly that. Standing up for righteousness is not always politically correct. Winning the battle does not always mean winning the war. So despite my valiant and successful efforts to protect my client, in the single stroke of a pen, almost everything I had was gone. My practice, the thousands of clients who trusted in my judgment, my income and, after a hard fought four year battle, so was my joy. What had started as a ministry in 1984, ended in the same way, fighting the good fight, doing all I could to protect a client and doing so by the rules. I had won the battle, but in the end, the system would win the war.

"Do not devise evil against your neighbor."

~ Proverbs 3:28

On April 3, 2003, I was presented with an unusual set of facts. Though red flags were waiving before my eyes, my inclination to help those in need kept me from turning away the woman crying in desperation. That decision set in motion a series of crucial events. It was that woman who ultimately changed the course of my life.

Through every facet of my career, I had always tried to follow the rules of man and to be obedient to the Word of God. In the end, doing so would serve me well. Though I faced one of the largest and most powerful law firms in the state, I knew my legal skill and faith in God was sufficient to defeat a fraudulent effort to force my client's home to foreclose. My client was the mother of the woman in tears. I was right on two counts. I should have heeded the red flags and I would ultimately defeat the fraudulent efforts.

With the help of a high priced lawyer, my client's neighbor had bound her to a sale contract, offering her far more than her house was worth; more, the evidence would later prove, than he was willing to pay. Unaware of my grasp of the law and dedication to my clients, the neighbor and his lawyer fought my every effort to close the deal before the foreclosure* - his chance to purchase the house for pennies on the dollar. His success would mean not only the loss of my client's residence, but her daughter and grandchildren's home as well. Both were in foreclosure. He and his attorney were confident their plan would work. They were wrong.

My client, having previously exhausted her bankruptcy remedies, had only one option to stop the foreclosures of both homes and close on the neighbor's contract. It was necessary to bring her mortgage current. With the mortgage company unwilling to compromise, the neighbor unwilling to close and with neither the time nor her credit standing sufficient to refinance, I sought to "loan" my client the roughly $10,000 she needed to stop the sale. It would be immediately repaid when she closed on the neighbor's deal. To do so ethically and to protect myself, I called the legal advisor of the Missouri Bar for advice.

Just one full business day prior to foreclosure, the Legal Advisor of the Missouri Bar finally returned my call and told me in no uncertain terms that I could not "loan" my client the money. No matter how dire the consequences nor how simple this solution, the Code of Professional Responsibility

16

clearly, in her estimation, said no. Instead she advised the only option provided by The Code was to purchase my client's house. Though not the optimum solution, and one not immediately even considered, my hands were tied. My client, an elderly woman, had no other choice if her homes were to be saved. In desperation to protect her equity I sought help from her family. None of her seven adult daughters, two of whom always accompanied her to my office, nor any of her family members could help. In my haste to help, I sought a friend who flipped houses. He chose to pass. I contacted a real estate agent to quickly locate a speculator. None could be found. I racked my brain for anything that would help. Long tired of the rich and powerful taking advantage of those less fortunate I knew I had the ability to help – and I did.

"Do not withhold good from those to whom it is due, when it is in the power of your hand to do so."

~ Proverbs 3:27

"Do not withhold good... when it is in your power to do so" was all that went through my mind. Needless to say, under the Code of Ethics I owed my client nothing more than vigorous representation, representation for which I had not sought payment despite her case precluding large amounts of income while I focused on her. But I had the ability to help above and beyond that typically extended by an attorney and to stand by doing nothing, allowing this woman to lose not only her home but the equity she appeared to have, as a Christian simply was not an option. Foreclosure would also have had the domino effect of losing her daughter's home and her car as well. Eight children and four adults would have been on the street. Everything hinged on saving her house.

From the day I started my law practice, I walked into my office each day not just as an attorney, but as a Christian first. My obligation was then, as it is now, first to the laws of God, then to the laws of man. God had been more than good to me, and failing to help someone who stood to lose so much did not fit within my Christian beliefs. With that in mind, though a risky proposition on several levels, I consulted a friend and pulled together the money to purchase the house in cash. This, after all, was the only way the Legal Ethics Counsel advised me I could help.

Like any other lawyer entering into a contingency contract with a client or real estate investor walking into a risky deal, the potential for profit or loss was discussed and put into writing. There was no time for an actual appraisal. The only valuations we had were two contracts clearly in excess of the value, the poor condition of the house and a verbal estimate provided by a real estate agent "if we changed the carpet and painted the walls." In reality, we had no interest in renovating the house. If we did, it would clearly need far more than a change of carpet and coat of paint. The windows were cracked, outdated and caked with layers of uneven paint. An inspection by a potential buyer had disclosed the need to completely rewire both of the two family units. The fixtures were destined to go. Such an additional investment would have been significant. Any increase in value, by every measure of law and industry practice, would go to us as buyers. Any loss, was ours as well.

18

With only hours before foreclosure, my client declined her right to retain another attorney, nor did she have the funds to do so. I asked for nothing in fees. Any attorney entering their appearance at that stage would need to be well versed in bankruptcy law, real estate and foreclosures. Though the bankruptcy had been filed, it was destined for dismissal. A new lawyer would have to be willing to take on two powerful law firms, appear in court the next morning, and do so without an ounce of pay. Hiring a new lawyer at this stage was not only unfeasible, it was her prerogative not to do so.

Just hours before the scheduled foreclosure the next day, I was able to retain a real estate law firm to draft a sales contract between my client and my friend and I as buyers. Later, I would seek out other attorneys to take on the battles she faced. None would bite. With my client having expressly waived her right to another attorney in writing and all other provisions of the Code of Professional Responsibility having been met, I thoroughly read and explained each provision of the contract with her and three of her adult daughters. During the reading, I made and had her initial several changes at her request, (providing that $2000 be paid to bring her car payment current and that I would make available another $5000 of escrowed funds so she could purchase another house. One of many legal decisions she made independent of my advice.) Still losing client fees, I continued to vigorously and successfully represent her to save her home. Having come from picking up my son from school, both he and the co-buyer were present. Her daughters signed as witnesses.

Since my client was still in bankruptcy and still under the neighbor's contract, both state and federal laws prohibited me from ethically taking possession of the house or even taking a deed. Technically the house belonged to the Bankruptcy estate and the right to purchase still belonged to the neighbor. Though I could have taken the deed, I did not. Our contract expressly subordinated our contract to his. As such, with absolutely no protection for the money extended, I paid off her entire mortgage, paid more than $2,000 in back car payments, and held in escrow the remaining funds. Stopping the neighbors unconscionable act, I nearly wiped out my bank account, enlisted a friend to borrow money,* and asked my mother to extend nearly all of her teacher's retirement.

Without a deed, security for the money extended was no more than reliance on simple human decency. It was unthinkable that anyone would not honor the trust being placed in them or appreciate such efforts made on their behalf. Or so I thought. After the bankruptcy was dismissed and the neighbor refusing to close on his contract, I realized I could at least have her sign over the deed. Unrecorded, it would remain subordinate to his right to close. Her response? "What deed?" The daughter who had benefited most from the transaction, now convinced my client not to sign over the deed. Even worse, shortly afterwards, I received an anonymous phone call from an attorney advising me that she and two of her daughters had visited his office in an effort to transfer the deed to her daughter. It was the daughter's intent to then make a loan and encumber the house with a new mortgage. The daughter would have had no obligation, and likely no intentions, of repaying the substantial down payment paid to save either home. The attorney was so appalled by her admission that I had saved her home from foreclosure by paying off the mortgage and trusted her

20

enough to have not taken a deed concurrently, that he was willing to betray the lawyer / client relationship and called to warn me. He had refused to be a part of their sinister act and had sent them on their way.

During the crucial appearance in bankruptcy court the following morning where the client was surrounded by no fewer than 60 attorneys, the mortgage was paid off and the foreclosure stopped. It was then that the truth of the neighbor's deal began to unfold. For a week his lawyer fought my every effort to close on his contract, even before our subordinate contract was written just hours before the foreclosure. Never intending to purchase my client's house for the inflated offer made, he was now stuck with closing. Nothing his lawyer did added up. Diversions seemed ridiculously contrived and every objection to closing was easily overcome. Yet they refused to close. Indeed, his lawyer filed a response to my Motion to Extend the Automatic Stay to halt the foreclosure, citing no fewer than 26 reasons why the motion should not be granted. In other words, despite having feigned an urgent desire to buy the house for a week while simultaneously providing barriers to doing so, suddenly the true objective came into view. Foreclosure. When I threatened them with a civil suit seeking punitive damages and legal fees which would be heard before an often generous city jury, they immediately jumped the gun and filed a suit for specific performance in the Court of Equity. Though my client ultimately agreed on her own to dismiss the lawsuit, their filing was smart nonetheless. The Court of Equity seats no jury. The judge and the judge alone makes the final ruling. Wielding the power of their law firm the outcome was almost certain.

Whoso returns evil for good, evil shall not depart from his house. "

~ *Proverbs 17:13*

When the dust finally settled after a five month legal battle, the neighbor succeeded in getting out of his overpriced deal. With me no longer representing the client, they both agreed to walk away; she with her mortgage free house, he free of paying an inflated price and damages for his fraud. He never adequately explained in his deposition, after having lived down the street from my client for over a decade, why he just happened along a week before a published foreclosure and offered her $40,000 more than he later admitted the house was worth. Nor did he explain why he directly approached my client with a second contract drawn up by his attorney, both knowing she was represented by counsel. The new contingencies would have guaranteed him a complete out when she breached one of the newly added terms. Dismissal of the neighbor's lawsuit came with the agreement that he not purchase the property.

With nearly $100,000.00 invested in money and legal time successfully protecting this client, (an unnecessary amount created by the neighbor's deceit and her own deception) it was now necessary to transfer the deed so the house could be listed for sale and reimbursement made. Little did my client know that most of my fees would have been waived as they were in many of my cases. In fact, the only billing statement ever presented to her was drawn up only after she reneged on transferring the deed and defaulting on the contract. Payment of my fees, as indicated in a letter to both my client and to the neighbor's attorney, were to be sought from the neighbor under his contract. Even the substantial majority of her bankruptcy fees had gone unpaid. Like the four other lawyers who represented her before me (a fact she had concealed), she had gotten hers and I had simply been had.

With the lawsuit dropped, the deed in her hands and a debt free house, although I had vigorously represented my client against these unscrupulous acts, did so without ever seeking a cent in fees up front, resolved two pending liens, had saved both her and her daughter's home from foreclosure, and her car from repossession, my client then used a bar complaint to circumvent transferring the deed. For the first time in twenty years of practice, I thought the neighbor had stooped to the lowest form of behavior I had seen. My former client, however, the one I had done everything above and beyond the call of duty to help, stooped even lower; a perfect opportunity for a powerful law firm to assure that their bitter, costly and embarrassing defeat would be vindicated. To add insult to injury, the original hearing on the Bar complaint was initially assigned to their office and a member of their firm to the panel. My request for change in venue and panel was initially ignored.

"He who justifies the wicked and condemns the just, both are an abomination to the Lord."

~ Proverbs 17:15

With his sites on the Office of Chief Disciplinary Council, months went by while the prosecutor dug for something, anything I had done wrong. Finding nothing, he finally filed a 93 paragraph Information (lawsuit); an age old tactic used by large firms who can afford to overwhelm opponents with work when the law and truth simply will not work. According to the Chief Hearing Officer later assigned to the case, the Information was the longest, by far, he had ever seen in his 17 years of handling bar complaints. I had won the battle, they would win the war.

Despite the effort to overwhelm me with allegations, the grace of God allowed me to persevere. Long hours of paid and pro-bono work had provided an income and client base far in excess of my need. With my youngest now away in school and a decision to serve on fewer boards, I rolled up my sleeves and prepared to take up the fight. The battle had just begun. It became obvious early in the process that nothing I said nor any evidence I produced would be sufficient to overcome their goal; not mounds of evidence, months of free legal representation, or eight pages of my client's contradictions I produced. Every effort to undermine me was used. In fact, the original filed complaint, riddled with inaccuracies on its face, was rewritten and submitted to both the panel and the Missouri Supreme Court. The original complaint, the one riddled with implausible allegations, was never presented to either. After all, it was not my client that mattered; it was the law firm that lost. I had stepped out of my place, and it was up to the Bar to make sure I stepped back in. Having terminated my right to a full hearing, physically ignoring my evidence and even attempting to intimidate me with misstatements of law, they recommended to the Missouri Supreme Court that I be disbarred. No consideration was given to the fact that two other law firms and six attorneys had assisted in either preparing the contract or attempting to enforce it. No one else was ever admonished, including the opposing firm who had engaged in multiple ethics violations.

Several days after receiving the recommendation of the panel, I received a call from the Missouri Supreme Court. Twenty six of my documents were missing from the evidence the Chief Disciplinary Council had submitted to the court; evidence neither the prosecutor, the Chief Hearing Officer nor any of the panel members had ever touched or listened to during the hearing. Clearly they had not ever reviewed my evidence before reaching the recommendation. *It was never in their possession.* Despite the Supreme Court rule pertaining to disciplinary proceedings, my right to a hearing to "continue from day to day" as necessary was thwarted. I was given an extremely limited opportunity to verbally present my case and my effort to submit evidence was rejected, the documents were literally left untouched on the table where I placed them before each member. Eventually I was abruptly told the next hearing, again scheduled a month apart, would be the last.

To further exacerbate the injustice, at no time during the entire process, including the Supreme Court hearing, were the words of the relevant Codes of Professional Responsibility ever read. Certainly they were never discussed. The most critical provision was so complex that a law journal article had been written about its ambiguities and the provision was later revised by the American Bar Association. My right to a trial as provided by Missouri law was simply ignored. The client never testified before the Court. I was denied the right to cross-examine her at trial.

After four years of legal wrangling I spent a full month on two hours of sleep per night writing my reply brief and aligning virtually every allegation with a document or deposed statement to discredit every false allegation levelled. No rock was left unturned. Despite answering every allegation, repeatedly discrediting my former client, pointing out the misconduct of the Prosecutor, Legal Advisor and Hearing Officer and producing mountains of evidence that refuted virtually every allegation that I had violated a single rule, more than four years after the original complaint was filed, my law license was suspended for three years.

Though the many facts of the case and relevant Rules of Professional Responsibility would have made an opinion invaluably instructive to the entire body of lawyers throughout the country, no opinion was written. No facts of the case, no opinion. No matter how legally skilled or how crafty, not a single word could have been written to justify the conclusion or support the order that was signed. In the end I was denied a full trial to which I was entitled and denied my license based on a 35 minute hearing. The suspension defied every rule of law and every ounce of evidence submitted.

Throughout the proceedings, evidence was lost and intentionally omitted, laws were misstated and ethics violated. Depositions that consistently corroborated my testimony were never used. Those I submitted were ignored. And yet, in the end, unsure that every other unethical tactic would be sufficient to win my disbarment, the prosecutor, who by then had succeeded in being elevated to Chief Disciplinary Council for the State of Missouri, actually stood before the Missouri Supreme Court in the first case he argued in that capacity and lied. Not misspoke, but knowingly lied

26

as an officer of the Court. Despite my successfully discrediting the Complainant (my former client and his only witness) over his objections and unequivocally proving she had lied about the most pivotal aspects of the complaint, the Chief Disciplinary Council for the State of Missouri repeated before the Court, the very allegation that the Chief Hearing Officer specifically ruled I had disproven. Making matters worse, the Chief Council waited to do so in his rebuttal, leaving no opportunity for me to respond. He successfully placed false and undue focus on me to cover up the numerous ethical violations of the lawyers who sought to take advantage of my client. Though the record compiled in my case disclosed gross misconduct on the part of those attorneys, to date, no action has been taken against them.

Having spent a life time trying to be as obedient to the laws of both God and man as humanly possible, and having gone well beyond the call of duty as an attorney, I entered into the disciplinary process believing the system would work and that truth would prevail. In fact, having been pulled into the process by a client who was so deceptive that her original complaint was unethically omitted from the record and rewritten to conceal her lies, I envisioned a moment when members of the Bar I had served for over 20 years would actually laud me for my valiant and successful efforts on her behalf. That was not to be.

"Though proud men smear me with lies, yet I keep your precepts."

~ *Psalm 119-69*

It seemed obvious from the questions asked during the 1/2 hour hearing that deprived me of the right to practice law, eliminated my entire source of income and tarnished my name, that none of the Missouri Supreme Court judges had ever reviewed all, if any, of the evidence submitted. Indeed, the Hearing Panel had not. No weight was given that I had impeached the only witness against me, provided a laundry list of civic, religious, community and educational boards I had served on for years, submitted mounds of evidence disproving misconduct on my part and cooperated with every phase of the proceeding. Abuse of power was brazen.

Per our United States Constitution, decisions of the Missouri Supreme Court, like the highest courts of all 50 states, are subject to review only by the US Supreme Court. As such, I appealed my case among the nearly 80,000 cases filed each year. But the country's highest court simply cannot hear them all. I was not seeking so much the reversal of the decision as I was the disclosure of the system's reckless, unethical and biased conduct. I had hoped an order would instruct other attorneys of the landmines they face. But my remedies were exhausted. The Missouri Supreme Court did not need to justify their order with an opinion, they rested confident that rarely will anyone appeal to the higher court or – if they do, that the case will be heard. Certiorari was denied.

"Count it all joy when you fall into various trials..."
~ James 1:2-4

In the spring of 2008, I sought to regain my joy by writing the book *21 Days to Joy, A Daily Devotional to Finding Joy.* Based on the psychological concept that you can change any behavior over a period of 21 days, I combined that concept with scriptural truths and focused on finding joy. With focused attention, much prayer and meditation on God's word, I did, indeed, regain my joy. Though my name had been disparaged by the false information printed on the Internet, including the Summary of the Case and my so-called response written by someone unknown to me, my perfect credit had been ruined and my home ultimately lost in foreclosure, my joy exceeded that I had ever known. Those who knew me knew better. True friends were made known.

Gone were the trips, the Mercedes and my son's college tuition. The majority of my furniture and possessions were sold in moving sales or donated to those less fortunate. My 16 year old cat had to find a new home; it was not feasible to bring her along. I watched helplessly as my clients were overcome with anger at the system, worry and in some cases despair. In the midst of this, teenagers of two of my clients attempted suicide; my clients forced to divide time between hospital beds and phone calls trying to resolve matters with an inexperienced attorney that would have taken me minutes. After making 58 payments on a 60 months bankruptcy plan, one woman simply let her case go. Losing all faith in the system, she had given up hope. Not knowing the consequences, I shared the story publicly for two years later discovering that at least two aspiring lawyers chose not to enter law school. They too had lost faith in the system.

I had lost faith in our system and respect for those who sat on the highest court of our state. Lawyers who took over my cases were overwhelmed with changes in the law and clients of their own. My experience far exceeded theirs, and issues I had resolved easily were suddenly battleground for dispute. Hundreds of people were hurt by the senseless acts of a neighbor, one client and a host of those we entrusted to the highest offices in our state.

"It was good for me to be afflicted, to learn your will."
Psalms 119:71

Despite the outcome, I learned lessons that would never have come any other way. I have met extraordinary people of faith and accomplishment I otherwise never would have met. I learned of the incredibly deep support of my children, my mother, my family and my friends. My faith in the power of God has increased tenfold, my freedom from the trappings of this world is all but complete and I have found exceeding joy in the abundance of God's gifts. His miracles never cease.

"What man intended for evil, God intended for good"
Genesis 50:20

Though the Powers-that-be had taken all that has value to man, they had only added immensely to those things that are of value to God. Yes, what man intended for evil, God intended for good.

As naïve as it might seem, fighting a major law firm, battling a broken system and learning that human decency fails at even the top, had been a daunting blow. I was exhausted, overwhelmed and isolated from it all. As I sat in my hotel room the night before my Supreme Court hearing, exhaustion and disappointment over took me. The pain felt when incorrectly thinking my husband had not called to encourage me, was the deepest I had ever felt. I had pushed him aside while treading furiously in treacherous, shark filled waters, and he in turn withdrew into himself. Though his missed call and message awaited me on my uncharged phone across the room, I felt the pain of a child whose parent had been falsely accused; a child whose parent had been taken away without so much as good bye, removed from his life for years. A child who likely will be evicted from his home, transferred to another school, lose contact with friends, go hungry more than once, become the target of gangs and preyed upon by desperate men. It was the pain of that child who, more likely than not, will drop out of school, will one day be imprisoned, will become addicted to drugs and will eventually inflict his trauma on others. It was through the piercing pain of that child and with an unwavering faith in God's unchanging love that The Ethics Project was born.

"And so, if we go out with this faith and with this determination to solve these problems, we will bring into being that new day and that new America."

Dr. Martin Luther King, Jr.

FOREWORD

There is much to consider about the current state of our society – about our morals, ethics, happiness, prejudices, love and hate; the system of incarceration we have come to know as replete with evil. Though the Bible tells us that God has imbued us with vast wealth, many are so consumed with acquiring more of man-made "things" that they fail miserably at seeing the miraculous beauty that unfolds before us every day. Even the darkest of night skies, indeed, because of the blackness of night, millions of stars paint the heavens in dazzling beauty. The moon evolves from night to night taking on new shapes and hues and positions itself across the universe, its light casts upon every child, woman and man regardless of their station in life. The most gallant attempt of even the most talented painter cannot exceed the extraordinary vision of the moon's light cast upon a river's face. It captivates us, those, that is, who see.

We have been blessed with trees of every shape and flowers of more colors and species than we can imagine. They grace our country's landscape from one end to the other, flanked by vast oceans of unparalleled splendor. The sun in its dazzling array of ever changing colors bestow us with decidedly breathtaking views both welcoming morning and bidding night goodbye. We have babbling brooks, majestic mountains, prairie lands and endless clouds. We are surrounded by songbirds, graceful swans, and unconquerable whales. Butterflies alight around us and the

32

winds bring music on invisible waves of air. And yet there is hate.

Despite the unlimited wealth of God given gifts, some continue on meaningless quests of greed, seeking material existences that unfailingly prove of no avail - the goal is unattainable, its thirst unquenchable, its acquisition a mere figment of imagined joy. And to the dismay of many, its pursuit results in relentless emptiness that seeks every source of fulfillment. Debt prevails, bank accounts swell, things and stuff accumulate, and yet the desire for more sends many on a relentless quest. Hearts are broken, disappointment grows, and doubt infuses every thought. The sense of failure to achieve not only the goals of the masses but those of the imagined – the perfect husband, the perfect wife, the perfect mother, son, daughter, friend and business person, ends in a desperate deluge of artificial cures. Demeaning others, inflicting physical and emotional pain, reducing someone else to a level lower than that in which one sees himself.

It is in this state of diminished self-esteem that the world unravels and those in the path of the denounced become footstools of moral corruption and targets of degradation. It is in this state, when joined by others, that a race of people becomes the intended victim of those who have lost their way; victims of those whose goal - happiness in those things that can never deliver on false promises, becomes an empty mirage.

While many have seemingly acquired much in the quest for the American dream, their vast acquisitions have seemingly obscured the reality of their lives. They are lost, empty, angry, confused, dismayed, hurt and most of all callous. In an effort to justify their choices that create mass suffering and dehumanize others, they not only use fear tactics to justify their actions but, as Dr. Joy DeGruy describes in her book, *Post-Traumatic Slave Syndrome[1]* they engage in cognitive dissonance. Cognitive dissonance, a theory of social psychology developed by Leon Festinger, is explained in his book, *When Prophecy Fails[2]* to be the process of reducing dissonance, or discomfort when an individual holds two conflicting beliefs. As applied to the profiteering that is part and parcel of mass incarcerations, those two conflicting beliefs are the pursuit of wealth through the imprisonment and maltreatment of other human beings and the underlying belief that such maltreatment flies in the face of an innate sense of good. The consequences of such an unfulfilled and conflicted life, has unfortunately, resulted in the abuse and degradation of millions subjected to their fall-out. The need to continually both feed and salve a consuming flame of greed, corruption and hate, evolved into an uncontrolled blaze that feeds on others and etiolates their own souls.

Long lists of failures, attempted solutions and gross injustices date back centuries and fill volumes of books. The contradictions of those who condemned the slaughter of African Tutsi women and children by Hutu warriors, the inhumane treatment of Chinese by a Communist China, the subjugation and murder of millions of Jews by Hitler's regime, the brutal reign of the Ayatollah and more recently the gassing of thousands in Syria, while creating murder, addiction and destruction in their own country are palpable. The castigation of foreign countries engaged in inhumane treatment of their own, deflects attention from the concurrent inhumane treatment of African Americans here in the United

34

States. Only those whose mental capacity is so altered by denial, could possibly point the finger at an entity across the sea while ignoring the three fingers pointing back at them. Chattel slavery, peonage, Jim Crow, and mass incarcerations as detailed in Michelle Alexander's seminal book, *The New Jim Crow*[3] make other oppressive societies look humane.

This book is not intended to be an exhaustive treatment of the state of incarcerations. It would be a daunting and unnecessary task to attempt to do what Michelle Alexander has already accomplished through years of extensive research and writing *The New Jim Crow*. Instead, *Incarcerations in Black and White* reflects a myriad of experiences and insights gained through practicing law in juvenile court, in private practice, through the disciplinary process previously shared and through thousands of interactions while establishing and expanding The Ethics Project. It attempts to take the reader through realities personally unknown before delving more deeply into the subject beginning in 2007. It assumes most are as unaware of and as uninvolved in the subject as I was before the glaring brokenness of this system gave me a shattering wakeup call. This book is an amalgamation of research, experience and commentary. Written after decades of unceasingly developing solutions to a broad range of problems, it attempts to move us from conversation to action.

One of the first things students are taught in law school is how to identify the issues relevant to a case. They are taught to carefully identify and study the facts of the case, and then define the core issues. Knowing those issues is the road map to success. For decades, law schools have used The Socratic

Method of study to hone the analytic skills of its students. The method has served well in teaching many to become successful, if not always, morally grounded lawyers. The Socratic Method, taken from the practice of Greek philosopher, Socrates, challenges the student with a series of questions intended to unearth contradictions in the original premise when answered. It is the method also used at Harvard Business School, a revered educational institutions that has produced thousands of CEOs now scattered across the corporate landscape.

More than a century following the emancipation of slaves, we read and hear legislators consistently articulate issues that fail to touch the core of the true problem. While curtly ignoring the determined factors that created conditions ripe for social upheaval and unlawfulness, law makers continue to throw billions of dollars toward research and useless remedies that do no more than put band-aides on gaping wounds – wounds continually reopened by policies designed to keep an entire class and race of people shackled to a downward spiral. We stand idly by and witness a country use prisons to recapture a lost economy, to focus more on punishment than habilitation. In-depth exploration of books like those previously mentioned, reveal the process of essentially re-enslaving African American men and women through the use of so-called Black laws, peonage, convict leasing and more recently through the "War on Drugs", three strike laws, zero tolerance and minimum sentencing.

It matters little to those whose storehouses are full that major cities and states verge on bankruptcy, that lives are ravaged or that the United States' primary economic advantage in the world, an educated citizenry, is quickly being lost. Once the world leader in education, the United States continues to fall in its ranking among other countries. According to recent reports the United States has fallen ten points in both high school and college graduation rates[4]. It now ranks 17th in the world, trailing even countries such as Germany and South Korea.[5] Without a well-educated populace, the United States will eventually fall in rank in other areas as well. If we are to move toward a more just society, one in which we seek to raise our children to be honest, morally fit, and responsible citizens and to correct rather than cage those we fail, it is imperative to first define the core issues. If we are to benefit from the wealth of talent of those who, for a myriad of reasons, are steered off track, we must analyze the problem with a goal of increasing our human capital rather than encaging them in concrete cells. Recent history has shown, however, that attempting to reverse a system that has been allowed to propagate incrementally and permeate virtually every aspect of society, would be akin to crafting a case similar to that of Wal-Mart Stores, Inc. v Dukes, et al.[6] The Walmart case is one encompassing so many plaintiffs and individual grievances in a class action lawsuit, that the mega-corporation's response was to seek dismissal because the case was too large to litigate.[7] Yet, like Wal Mart's team of highly skilled executives and lawyers who manage over 9200 stores, 2,000,000 employees worldwide and generate hundreds of billions of dollars each year, there will be those who resist reformation of a broken system claiming they cannot navigate a path to success. When the very system that needs retooling generates billions of dollars to buy lawyers, influence legislators and persuade judges with crafty yet implausible arguments, the challenge of doing what is morally and ethically correct becomes daunting.

But we cannot, like learned judges and impotent legislators have often done, cave-in to the massive undertaking that lies ahead, acquiescing to the exploitation of those human souls. We must tackle this affliction of greed head on, deciphering and indeed embracing the significance of the enormous task. The road that lies behind us, more importantly, the road that lies ahead, requires that we face and understand the pathology of hate in those who inflicted so many wounds on generations of Native Americans, African Americans, Japanese, Hispanics, Chinese, Jews, Haitians and Muslims. Until we start directing federal and state dollars into the hands of minorities to study the cancerous cells of greed and racial hatred that continues to ravage this country through those with power, history will be repeated.

Indeed healing requires that we acknowledge the complicity of many within the afflicted race; Jews who profited from the purchase and sell of Blacks in the same manner as those who persecuted them,[8] African natives who led unsuspecting tribesmen to doomed destinies aboard ill-fated ships, Colored slaves who abandoned a code of silence to gain Massa's favored hand, Negroes who brown nosed their way to the glass ceiling, if, indeed they got that close, and Afro Americans who filtered drugs into their brothers' veins and sold their sisters' bodies. There are Native Americans who traded their souls to gain illicit interests in casinos on segregated land, shamelessly amassing wealth by lending heritage to underhanded deals.[9] And as with those of other hues, Hispanics and Chinese are not without those who

38

parted ways with their race and formed alliances with the enemy; they too have shared in the affliction of their fellow man. A portion of shared guilt belongs to all.

And the enemy? Though "the man" has been blamed for every social ill from filtering drugs into Black communities to crafting school curriculums devoid of historical truth, the term as used by a broad spectrum of African Americans seldom blankets the entire white race. Many would agree that "the man" has no universal definition, though many would agree that having "white" skin would be found somewhere in most descriptions. "The man" is not limited to gender, with more and more women wielding as much power as men, it transcends any particular group.

Within the church, the enemy would be seen as "principalities". To others it is anyone who has and wields power wrangled from one nationality through war and destruction. Native Indians fell by the onslaught of bullets, the Chinese to the infusion of opium and unjust laws.[10] Jews were trampled and starved. The Japanese were interred and Haitians turned back to drown. Hispanics were stopped at the border and African Americans stolen, beaten and enslaved. Generation after generation every measure of might and injustice has been used to establish and overtake with dominance.

There are whites who marched alongside Dr. Martin Luther King Jr., those who fought on the front lines in the fight for racial justice. Many even died securing the rights of others. There are Schwerner and Chaney, two young, white students who miscalculated the depth of racial hatred in the South. Their presence did not quell the heated protest against the Black vote, but fueled a flame that resulted in their heinous deaths.[11] There were Catholic nuns and priests who broke lock step with the Catholic Church[12] – an entity that too often turned its collective heads to the injustices of the day and, in fact, too often engaged in discriminatory practices itself.[13] There are those who led battles, wrote tomes, and risked their own safety to harbor runaway slaves in the Underground Railroad. And there were white judges, police, historians and more who resisted racist calls of hate. They marched to the beat of different drummers and rose in resistance to the climate of the day.

If not "them" then who? Was the breadth of complicity in the degradation of Blacks so egregious that few will claim their rightful place? So it appears. Though openly engaged in brutal and brazen acts of discrimination and abuse, the growing practice of the day is to deny such acts took place. According to some, the institution of slavery was no more than a gentile institution that saved Black Africans from the desolate lives they knew. For slave owners, it was considered both a Christian right and duty to subdue the wild mannerisms of their slaves and teach them their civility.[14] But education was a different thing. As noted in the *Warmth of Other Suns* by Isabel Wilkerson, a white supremacist, gubernatorial candidate campaigned against the education of Blacks stating, "[t]he only effect of Negro education is to spoil a good field hand and make an insolent cook." He was eventually sent to the Senate.[15]

Amnesia has set into the minds of those whose current wealth is inextricably tied to the free labor of Blacks. Indeed, some who have a faint recollection of the practice of slavery claim that ownership was an onerous expense. According to them, slaves were costly. They had to be housed, fed, clothed and cared for when sick.[16] No matter how poorly the aforementioned was grudgingly performed, the descendants of slave owners seem to remember only these intrusions on their privileged lives, a lifestyle gained only through the blood, sweat and tears of Black men, women and children. The wealth they accumulated, the plantation mansions they built, the lavish parties they threw and grand clothing they wore seemed to have little, if any, connection to the ceaseless days of brutally hard work of slaves.

Fast forward to the 21st Century and the reality of slavery has been sanitized in textbooks and classrooms. While no apology seems to be in view, the mere fact the staggering truth has, for decades been all but omitted from American history, is proof positive that an apology is due. Omitted are images of children being ripped from the arms of their mothers and sent off to plantations miles away. Omitted is mention of the mutilations exacted as punishment for a slave's failure to comply with even the most oppressive demands. Omitted are depictions of bodies hanging from trees, tarred, burned or brutalized. Rarely if ever will there be mention of the routine rape of countless women and girls or of male slaves beaten for rebuffing the advances of white mistresses of the house. Little is mentioned of 40 Acres and a Mule. So brutal was the treatment of the men and women who secured the economic foundation of this country[17] that the physical ramifications of their sacrifice was permanently recorded in their bones.[18] Yet, little will be found in the text of students' books.[19] Indeed, in 2010, what little reference is made to the institution of slavery in Texas school books, the Tea Party has demanded be removed.[20]

The savage treatment of slaves, justified by assignment of sub-human status, denote debase and elevated self-images often reflected in pathologies existing in the American way of life. The children that suckled at the breasts of Black slaves have given birth to generations that continue the tradition of casting aside their own; attempting to replace human emotion and touch with elite boarding schools, high end cars and expensive clothes. Throughout generations they continue to fill empty souls with material wealth; larger homes, bigger boats, and grander style. They build skyscrapers of brick that grant no more benefit than The Tower built in Bable; the builders speaking a common language of greed. So busy in such pursuits they have yet to understand their souls have become more vacant, the vapid emptiness yet to be filled.

Even the church became complicit in this charade of sin, trading indulgences of known wrongs for a sufficient payment of cash.[21] Cash for coveting, money for whore mongering, thousands for theft. Pay enough to the church and any amount of sin could be forgiven, after all such power of forgiveness was given through the Papacy. Or was it? Such behavior on the part of those purportedly called and ordained by God most certainly created a tradition of disregarding the precepts of His word by engaging in any level of intemperateness for the cost of an offering. The bigger the sin the bigger the buck.

It is inconceivable that one could read and believe in the Holy Bible and find interpretations that suited their flesh. It was the Bible itself that called for one to denounce such indulgent behavior and find peace, joy and happiness in the comfort of the Risen Christ. But such adherence to both the

42

precepts of God's words and its rich blessings and promises were often cast aside for immediate wealth. Scriptures that mandated fidelity to one's spouse meant nothing to a man of means who had unfettered access to any number of slaves. The admonition to be Christ like and good meant nothing more than a pretense of holiness when the church bell rang, the choir began to sing and the collection plate was passed. Then and only then did one feign such pious behavior, putting on airs and dismissing every notion of wrong doing.

"The peculiar institution" as it is referred to in the book by the same name,[22] was even justified by specific texts within the Bible, twisted, and misinterpreted in whatever manner that suited the end result. Preachers preached from the pulpit the moral duty of their congregations to subdue the Negro slave and use them efficiently to establish economic prowess. Wives were hoodwinked by their husbands or simply turned the other cheek rather than lose benefit of their Southern comforts. They possessed little more power than the young slaves who warmed their husband's feet. They eagerly accepted implausible explanations that Negro children had taken on their master's features and assumed their color simply by association and assimilation. When awareness of such explanations became undoubtedly less than true, these scorned women of privilege brutalized their husbands' darker seeds, often resulting in death.

To further assuage the act of enslaving, over working and brutalizing the African slaves and to protect themselves from the usual consequences of such acts, laws were enacted that removed any threat of guilt, trial or punishment for a slave owner, or anyone else at his direction, to kill a slave. Citing the State of Virginia's Casual Killing Act of 1669, Joy

DeGruy discusses this phenomenon of dehumanizing slaves using the legislative process.[23]

> *And if any slave resist his master, or owner, or other person by his or her order, correcting such slave, and shall happen to be killed in such correction, it shall not be accounted a felony; but the master, owner and every such other person so giving correction, shall be free and acquit of all punishment and accusation for the same, as if such accident had never happened.*

For Christians, the admonition that "Thou shalt not kill" became only a mere suggestion. Indeed, the heinous murders of innocent Black children were justified by designating them as less than human. The existence of such laws provided a backdrop for a myriad of capricious laws enacted through decades of all white, all male legislative bodies. With no input from those being governed, laws were and many are to this day, written, discussed and passed with a singular goal in mind, the continued economic superiority of those who do the writing and the subjugation of those who create their wealth. Provisions are bantered back and forth in a volley of compromises serving no other purpose than to arrive at mutually beneficial goals. You scratch my back, I'll scratch yours.

Laws are written to create financial gain – and before they are passed by legislative vote, corporations spring up to reap the profit. "Insider trading" applies only to Securities not to influence on Congressional votes. Laws related to crime gain support through fear mongering among the voting public and payment to those who wrangled legislative seats. Backroom deals explain why crime reported by the media increased

44

threefold, from 571 stories to over 1600 between 1991 and 1993, according the book *The Perpetual Prison Machine*.[24] Not surprisingly polls show that Americans viewed crime as the country's biggest problem[25] just as prison populations (and therefore, profits) were beginning to stave off.[26] What better way to convince Congress to increase prison allocations than to have frightened constituents demand something be done. Money is peddled through the halls of Congress though "In God We Trust" is rarely seen. Gone are the days when cold hard cash was slid into slim, white envelopes and craftily slipped from one hand to another. The process has become more sophisticated and bolstered by the U.S. Supreme Court ruling Citizens United v. The Federal Election Commission[27] that effectively designated corporations as people for the purposes of donating to political candidates. Only in the wake of financial prowess could such a revered institution deem a legal fiction the equivalent of human beings and grant "corporations, associations and unions constitutional protections.

Many of the laws themselves, those that lines the pockets of its proponent, serves as a thinly veiled attempt to help the poor. Funds are set aside to award minorities small contracts that ultimately rely on supplies and labor from majority owned firms. While low-income housing is a welcome presence in previously depressed neighborhoods, mansions are built in suburbs from the profits they reap. It is the contract that has real value, not the housing that they build. Even when set-aside programs designate a percentage of the work for minority firms, an even greater portion goes into the pockets of wealth, white men. In almost all circumstances, the vast majority of supplies used will directly or indirectly benefit the Haves far more than the

Have-nots. Free cell phones, medical supplies, food stamps and clothes, while heralded in minority neighborhoods as advantageous gifts, do little or nothing to create jobs or wealth for the recipients. They pour the "kool aid" and the masses drink it in.

Other laws fill the pages of countless books, restricting the freedom of some while simultaneously creating a path to prison. Legislation known as "Black Codes" were given birth immediately after the emancipation of slaves. Laws were enacted that criminalized even the most benign acts. Using obscene language, vagrancy or selling cotton after dark[28] could land a freed Black man in jail. Failing to cross the street when a white man approached could buy a Black man or woman time in jail. Failing to show proof of employment immediately after having been freed as a slave would find them arrested, fined and farmed back out, often to the same owner from whom they had been released. Years of hard labor did little to gain freedom from costs that continued to mount. Court fees, sheriff's fees, food, and shelter. An endless nightmare of costs, that by law, were charged, demanded and used to endlessly extend enslavement. The entire purpose to confine men to labor camps and benefit from their work.[29]

Blackmon's exhaustive analysis of convict leasing also gives insight to the common practice of peonage that Joy DeGruy also describes in *Post Traumatic Syndrome*.[30] Much like so-called payday loan companies that bind borrowers with interest rates legally exceeding 500%, peonage kept freed men bound to white employers until their "debts" were paid in full. Because food, housing and clothing would typically be added to the original debt, it was often impossible for workers to ever be free. Failure to pay even exaggerated debts was justification for jail. Thanks to legislators both now and then, millions of men and women remained perpetually indebted to the peonage system a century ago and to payday loan companies today.

In the centuries that have past, seemingly unconquerable achievements have been gained. The United States and Russia put men on the Moon, the Third Reich was overthrown and the Berlin Wall destroyed. Against all odds both slavery and lawful segregation ended and methods of communicating around the world in seconds have evolved. For many, if not all, the most astonishing event of all has been the election of an African American man to the Office of President of the United States. Indeed, both his lineage and his name made such a feat seem impossible.

An incalculable number of impossible feats have proven to be possible. In many instances lives were lost. In others, hearts were changed. In each, dedicated and determined individuals acknowledged a need for change and courageously led the fight. To have looked the other way, to have buried their heads in the sand would have meant decades more of oppression, hatred, brutality, injustice, and loss of freedom for millions. To have ignored the anguish of children and the pleas of adults would have meant a nation destined for destruction.

There are times throughout history, when men and women have stood strong. When they have refused to point fingers at other nations while ignoring the problems at home. There are times when a handful of committed individuals have simply said, enough. They have refused to submit to a tyranny of greed. They have refused to accept a self-proclaimed righteousness of a class of people and have faced an uphill battle to dismantle a system that not only destroys the lives of targeted individuals but has claimed the soul of a nation.

There are times throughout history when men and women are moved to act. When the necessity for revolt is implicit in the evil that continues to prevail. There are times in history, when all are called to accept a degree of personal discomfort to demand fairness and justice for those who cannot fight. There are times in history when the masses join together and vow to endure the fight until every person is free of hate and injustice.

This is such a time.

Chapter 1
THE GREAT EXCEPTION

"Ain't I a man?" ~ *Dred Scott*

On December 6, 1865, The United States Congress adopted the 13th Amendment to the United States Constitution. Although Delaware, Kentucky, Missouri, and New Jersey were the only states that maintained legalized slavery at the time, the apparent intent of that amendment was to abolish slavery throughout all existing states. Like the Missouri Compromise, however, its enactment was clearly the result of concessions made between abolitionists and slavery proponents. The carefully chosen language that comprises Section 1 of the Amendment, signifies no intention to obliterate the "peculiar institution". It did, instead, set the stage to merely transfer logistics. Though the United States has been touted as a free and civilized society, Congress reserved the right to maintain slavery and involuntary servitude as punishment for crimes.

Section 1. Neither slavery nor involuntary servitude, except as a punishment for crime where of the party shall have been duly convicted, shall exist within the United States, or any place subject to their jurisdiction.[31]

Despite the unambiguous language of Section 1, it remains a well-accepted premise that slavery has been abolished in the United States. Recitation of the 13th

Amendment has typically excluded the one exception- "except as a punishment for crime where of the party has been duly convicted." Innocent enough in its tone yet calamitous in its application. With little passage of time, the definition of crimes began to evolve. Laws emerged that targeted the newly freed Blacks and the term "duly convicted" gave way to errant juries, false witnesses and aberrant judges.[32] Notwithstanding indentured servants who continued to work under conditions not much better than that of slaves, Blacks were quickly re-enslaved via the same constitution that had set them free. Newly enacted laws required freed Blacks to enter into onerous contracts for employment and for various spurious reasons many would be convicted. Under the 13th Amendment, those "duly convicted" of "crimes" often were consequently leased out to companies or the very owners that had been forced to set them free.[33]

With the 13th Amendment dismantling one the most profitable institutions in the United States, nearly 150 years after the "abolishment of slavery" the United States now leads the entire world in the percentage of its citizens incarcerated at any given time. One in every 100 people in the United States are currently confined to prisons or jails. Millions more remain restricted by probation or parole, limited by the employment available. While some sit idle in overcrowded cells, many are used for labor for which meager wages are paid. Tax payers cover the cost of both. While the paychecks of common citizens are tapped, millionaires are made from the construction of prisons and provision of goods and services. Every year over fifty billion tax dollars ($50,000,000.000) are spent to build and maintain state prisons alone.[34] Additionally, nearly eight billion federal tax dollars ($8,000,000,000) are spent on federal corrections, exclusive of its Federal Prison Industries, UNICOR. Like private industries, the vast majority of the income produced benefit those who manage and provide goods and services.[35]

Though the overall rate of incarceration is a deplorable commentary on the United States, even more disturbing is the disparity in the number of Black men occupying prison cells. According to The Human Rights Watch, the rate of incarceration of Black men in the State of Minnesota, is 23 times that of whites. In Maryland, Black men make up an astonishing 79% of the prison admissions, though African Americans are less than 30% of the general population.[36] Though five times as many whites use drugs than African Americans, African Americans are incarcerated ten times more frequently for drug offenses than whites.[37] To date, one in every ten Black men in the United States are under some form of correctional supervision and one in six has been incarcerated since 2001.[38] Needless to say, the voting rights provided by the US Constitution are impacted by convictions, further diluting the rights of Blacks.

As reported in The National Journal, there is an estimated six million people, 2.5 percent of the population, that are ineligible to vote due to felony convictions, the majority of who have served their time but remain on probation or parole.[39] Citing a state by state analysis by The Sentencing Project, The Journal noted that Alabama, Florida, Kentucky, Mississippi, Tennessee and Virginia, all southern states, have disenfranchised more than 7% of their populations

51

through use of incarcerations with Florida and Virginia exceeding 20%.[40] Even more telling of the racial motivation behind voter disenfranchisement is that 13 percent of African American men have lost the right to vote due to convictions, seven times higher than the national average.

While skillfully using only 26 words that now decimate entire communities, Congress included nothing in the Constitution to address the problems this amendment would create. Consideration of the children left behind, the parent left to raise them, the family torn apart or the community left in its wake were omitted. The ramifications are immeasurable. It is with the children in mind, indeed, the entire African American and other marginalized communities, that attention must be drawn to the impact the full language of the 13th Amendment has had on our communities. It is imperative to arouse the realization that slavery is alive and well in the United States and is sanctioned by our very Constitution. Slavery is abolished *"...except as punishment for crimes..."*

Slavery continues to be a word so wrought with pain and indignation that the correlation must be made between its use prior to its abolition (in the cotton fields) and its current use as an economic tool and major source of labor within the walls of prisons. It is imperative to give visual and visceral meaning to the decision of legislators and businessmen to continue profiting from contrived laws, over-zealous and wrongful prosecutions, and to awaken those who comfortably distance themselves from this issue.

The collateral effects of imprisonment on our society is incalculable. The inauthentic use of concrete cages as punishment for those who violate laws often enacted with the calculated intent of perpetuating the benefits of slavery are too often a shameful reality in this country. Indeed, many state and national laws are circumspect at best when viewed from the lens of race. Many deride the disparity in sentencing for those convicted of use or possession of crack cocaine as opposed to powered cocaine, but many other instances exist as well. Indeed, the 2010 attempt to correct the gross injustice of sentencing between crack cocaine and powered cocaine was telling. The original law that had resulted in those convicted of laws involving crack cocaine (an illegal substance for which African Americans are 85% more frequently convicted) being sentenced at a rate 100 times more severely than those convicted of violations involving the same quantity of powered cocaine (an illegal substance used mostly by whites) ended in a compromise that merely narrowed the sentencing disparity to 17 times more severe for crack rather than simply making the law fully equitable.[41]

Black school children are routinely suspended or expelled from school while their white counterparts involved in the same incident go unpunished. This practice exists despite (or because) of evidence that suspensions have a long term outcome that increases the chance of future incarceration.[42] There is also the fact that white men have run shirtless in public parks for decades and are allowed to be scantily dressed in public, but young Black men who allow their pants to sag can now be arrested for doing so.[43] White students admit to stashing caches of drugs beneath their beds and doctors dispense them with regularity to the Hollywood elite, but seldom are arrests made. In contrast, Black students are routinely searched and arrested for minimal amounts of marijuana. Charlie Sheen could flagrantly display what appeared to be drug addiction and likely drove under the influence. No news reports show he was ever followed, stopped, searched or arrested for possession or tested for any drugs. Whites of any age are free to traverse any road in America yet Blacks are frequently stopped, searched and escorted out of town when venturing too far from home. That is if they are lucky. It is not unusual that Black youth and their cars are illegally searched, pulled from cars simply for "driving while Black". Though laws grant the right to refuse a search of your person or vehicle, in reality the failure to consent often results in additional harassment or scrutiny. Drugs have been planted and in instances where nothing can be found or planted,[44] young, Black males are taunted until their tempers are no longer constrained. Even when cooperating with officers who take matters too far, often dire consequences result.[45]

Certainly, in the instance of Harvard Professor, Henry Louis Gates[46] and much more tragically, Amadou Diallo, even approaching their own homes raised the suspicion of police. In the case of 22 year old Diallo, an unarmed, West African immigrant, the result was four police officers riddling his body with 17 of 41 bullets fired. Mr. Diallo was doing nothing more than reaching for identification.[47]

Hatred persists in this country and it is codified in the U.S. Constitution. While the 13th Amendment looks innocuous on its face, saving untold numbers of slaves from slavery, it was merely a compromise to allow the re-enslavement of Blacks and others using crime as a pretext for confinement and work. Through the use of that one "exception" an entire prison industry evolved and millions upon millions have been convicted of what some admittedly call harmless crimes. Often quoted only in part, the 13th Amendment not only provides a loophole for injustice, it gave Congress the power to enact laws to enforce it.

Section II: Congress shall have power to enforce this article by appropriate legislation.[48]

And enforce it, it does.

Inarguably, every ounce of wealth in this country is inextricably tied to the labor of Black slaves. To the extent Blacks have continued to be trafficked through state, federal and privately run prisons, nothing will ever be achieved in this country that is not attributed to the labor and contributions of African Americans. That African Americans continue to be denied full enjoyment of the country their labor built, is an enduring travesty. It is a travesty attributed to the failure of the Founding Fathers to include broad protections against slavery and involuntary servitude when drafting and enacting the U.S. Constitution and to modern congressional bodies who have codified and sustained an industrial setting in which human beings are effectively used for slave labor. The treatment of Americans confined to prisons today are scant different from the treatment of slaves in the past. Neither bear any resemblance to the humane standards demanded for citizens in other countries.

A cruel and evil system has been created, not by those who the self-righteous call criminals but by the very government we empower to serve. Generations of children and adults have been labeled as criminals and thereby legally enslaved. The emoluments of creating a culture of poverty, disease, unemployment and destruction, has been a burgeoning system of prisons for profit. The reward for evil has been jail cells filled with those who self-medicated, acting out of unresolved pain and anger toward a system of injustice and denial. It has been the laws that marginalized them and denied them employment then imprisoned them for trying to survive. Congress had the power to enforce the 13th Amendment and could have done so for the good. It could have enacted laws to employ rather than imprison, to educate rather than convict. Better late than never.

Chapter 2
FROM THE COURT STEPS TO NASDAQ

"He who commits injustice is ever made more
wretched than he who suffers it."

~ *Plato*

Over the 150 years since the 13th Amendment was ratified, there has been a relentless effort to use the carefully worded law to replace the economy lost when slavery ended. The social implications of that tainted construct has been immeasurable. For more than a century, individuals have been empowered to recklessly write and use laws to accuse the innocent and banish them to work.[49] Legislators have bastardized the process and enacted laws that reached far beyond the boundaries of reason. They have falsely accused men of crimes they did not commit and over sentenced others for the ones they did. Once in their control they worked many in mines, factories, steel mills and on railroads often until their death.[50] With each passing year, those who lost the long and bitter war to retain a certain way of life, have continued to manipulate the language of the 13th Amendment to imprison, abuse, castigate, banish, disenfranchise, segregate, demoralize, punish and weaken countless African Americans, Hispanics and poor whites. Despite many years of debate and legislation, more African Americans are incarcerated, under probation or parole or still suffering the vestiges of incarceration today than were enslaved at the time the 13th Amendment was ratified.

Long used as a means of replacing a lost economy, prisons have also served as a form of eugenics. With the ever increasing population of children serving life sentences, and adults sentences constantly lengthened, those incarcerated in the prime of their lives are effectively denied their reproductive rights. Though no longer the law today, at one point Virginia's "Eugenic Sterilization Act", which was adopted by more than 30 states and copied by Nazi Germany, mandated the compulsory sterilization of any person in a Virginia institution who was "insane, idiotic, imbecile, or epileptic". Their reproductive rights were lost forever.[51] Of course, the determination of such status was left to arbitrary discretion. As arcane as such laws may seem today, some states continued the practice as late as the 1970s.[52] In the 21st Century, the same result is essentially achieved by confining millions to institutions during the prime of their lives and segregating them from members of the opposite sex. Sentencing guidelines established in the 1980s and discriminately applied to minorities, have resulted in life terms for African American teenagers at a rate 50% more frequently than whites committing the same crimes. Such sentences inhumanely deny them the basic human right to ever reproduce.[53] Even those with less than life sentences are released from prison long after their prime reproductive years. Women, many who remain in prison through menopause,[54] often lose the ability to have children all together.

Even those who already have children when entering prison may lose them before their release. Under the

Adoption and Safe Families Act (ASFA) enacted by Congress and signed into law by President Clinton in 1997, parental rights can be terminated when the child of an incarcerated person has been in foster care for 15 of the previous 22 months.[55] Since the average prison sentence well exceeds 22 months, there is a strong possibility of an incarcerated parent permanently losing their parental rights and a child being adopted out.[56] This practice illustrates another instance in which modern law mocks that of pre-emancipation slavery when it was common practice to break up slave families, separating husbands from wives, parents from children, and siblings from siblings, sending each of them off to different plantations miles away.[57]

With a large percentage of African American men already imprisoned and women being the fastest growing segment of prison population increases, terminating parental rights of prison inmates can often mean the child permanently loses both parents. Such an outcome is the potential reality for as many as one-fourth of African American children, since one in four have at least on parent in prison at some point during their childhood. (Up from one in seven since 1978.)[58] According to the Sentencing Project, in 2009 there were 1.7 million children with a parent in prison, an 81% increase in 15 years.[59] Seventy percent (70%) of those children were African American.[60] The percentage of incarcerated mothers increased by 122% in that same period.[61] Though statistical data reflects a negative impact on children who often have not only lost a father to incarceration but increasingly a mother as well, this conclusion will be left to common sense.

Human Trafficking in the Name of Crime

From the time the slave trade began, when human beings were stolen from their homeland, deemed to be property and sold on courthouse steps, there has been only defacto change in the act of choosing, labeling and treating certain Black men, women and children as property. As previously noted, there are as many Blacks today who suffer the restrictions and vestiges of confinement as there were during the last days of slavery. Indeed, to some degree, the slaves who catered to the needs of their owners in 1865, experienced more freedom then than the men and women in prisons today. Unlike those entrapped in today's system, slaves were not confined to concrete cages with steel bars. As barbaric as were the conditions back then, today's conditions are barbaric as well.[62]

In many ways those who are trafficked in prisons today are exploited in frighteningly similar way as slaves. With 100% of able-bodied federal prisoners required to work, many are lured into the Federal Prison Industries where they are paid as little as 40¢ an hour to produce billions in goods and services. Those who work in the prison itself are paid little more than $1.00 a day. In today's dollars these inmates, regardless of where they work, receive less than that of newly freed slaves in 1865.[63] The meager wages paid to victims of this unjust system is further evidence of the ill intent of those who conceived of and perpetuate a system that generates millions of dollars in profit. There is virtually no difference in the work done by those imprisoned today, a disproportionate number who are African American men and women, and those who were forced into convict leasing under similarly false or disparately applied charges. Now just as then, a staggering number are innocent of the crimes for which they have been convicted yet are forced into labor as well.[64] A blueprint of yesterday's system, they both fulfill a common purpose; fill prison beds and increase prison profits.

Even assuming the guilt of the many confined, the conditions under which these men, women and children are forced to live place the United States among societies of much lower strata and not far above the slave holders of old. Billy clubs now replace the whips and the chains are merely newer. They are clothed better only because it puts money into the pockets of someone else. But overall, the systems remains the same. Like the 10,000 individuals sentenced as youth to life sentences without the possibility of parole[65] (the ones who will die within prison walls) even the men and women who are guilty as charged are the ones who society failed the most. Having failed them as children, society once again turns its head while they are subjected to years of brutality, confinement, emotional neglect and sexual improprieties. Primitive at best.

Life Sentences: Even for the Young

As the only country in the world that allows children and teenagers to be sentenced to prison for life without the possibility of parole[66] there is a glimmer of hope for the thousands of children serving life sentences. The U.S. Supreme Court issued a series of cases intended to protect juveniles from an overzealous system. In the first case, the Court made it unconstitutional to sentence a person to death for a crime committed as a juvenile.[67] In another case it was deemed unconstitutional to sentence a person under the age of 18 to life in prison without the possibility of parole in non-homicide cases.[68] And in two similar cases, the Court held that mandatory death penalties, even for homicide, were unconstitutional as constituting cruel and unusual punishment if committed by juveniles.[69] Even so, those whose stock prices rely on the number of juveniles placed in their custody, laws are enacted and unjustly enforced to assure a maximum return. The wheels of justice are slow.

Much like the African slaves who died in bondage and never saw their freedom, so is the fate of more than 159,520 individuals currently serving life terms. According to a study conducted by the Sentencing Project, a large percentage of those serving life sentences were convicted of non-violent offenses, not homicides or other heinous acts as one might think.[70] Not surprisingly, the majority of those sentenced are African American, a disturbing 62%.[71] The more than 10% increase in life sentences and the more than 22% increases in life sentences without possibility of parole, is indicative of the same guaranteed income that came with owning slaves. The longer the sentence the more that is earned. Small investment, big return.

Like the larger society that paid the moral and financial cost to support the lifestyle of millionaires during the pre-emancipation system of slavery, it is the modern taxpayer who foots the bill today. Every year those who work and struggle to support their own families are forced to pay the cost of over 2 million prisoners every year (nearly 170,000 of them for life) at the average cost of $28,893.[72] (Yet, another increase from 28,262 the previous year.[73]) Add in the rising cost of medically maintaining an aging populace, and those who profit from these excessive sentences are guaranteed even more. Life sentences serve no other interest than the interest of those who are paid.

Consistent with other anomalies occurring since 1865, the slave traders of today have created a sophisticated system of involuntary servitude and subjugation. Elevated to Wall Street trading, stock prices are determined by the number of beds they fill, essentially placing a price on the head of every man, woman and child they convict. The longer the stay the higher the stock. Unlike bloodhounds that ran through swamps and southern moss looking for frightened slaves, those who profit from prisons today simply make phone calls, have drinks, or chat while playing golf. They plot ways to gain their prey over Cohibas and a stiff drink, replacing bloodhounds and bounty hunters with police. They create new laws, require mandatory time, and issue longer sentences. None of which has anything to do with safety.

One Way or Another

No longer plying their trade on courthouse steps, those who would sooner see a nation destroyed than lose a stock point, plan, plot, deceive and bribe. Their hi-tech system of corruption, greed and exploitation is so vast that few politicians or legislative bodies say no. They have given capitalism a new spin and scare the public into believing they have made it safe. The depth of hatred and insensitivity has exceeded even that of the barbaric nature of those who whipped and beat and auctioned human life. They will sit in pews on Sunday morning and check stock prices the very next day. They no longer stand on dusty roads or courthouse steps fending off the hot sun or pouring rain while auctioneers cry their sales. They no longer have Black men, women and children lining cobblestone streets waiting for the highest bid. Today they have reached an all-time low where they effectively sell their primary commodity, prison beds filled by human beings, on the stock exchange. White or Black, just as long as they are filled. They ravage the lives of men and women and leave devastation in their wake. Those they lock away for as little as $30 in marijuana are those who over a million children call mom or dad, that many call son, daughter or even granddad. They place a price on the heads of those swept off the street by overzealous police,[74] prosecuted by self-seeking prosecutors[75] and sentenced by judges either unable to circumvent mandatory laws and step down from the bench[76] or themselves a part of the greed.[77] They take their prey miles from family, friends and familiar faces and build up towns where more fortune awaits. They take away the vote their ancestors bombed, shot and lynched to keep, and shift census counts where their interests lie. Black communities not only lose thousands of lives but thousands of votes as well. Census counts direct federal dollars away from communities where prison populations are derived and direct them to the community where the prisons are built. Lose-lose, win-win. They have devised a system that seems perfect on all counts, except that it paves a road to hell lined with lost children, broken hearts, ravaged lives and empty souls. There, the money gained will have no value and their pleas will go unheard. When the Constitution said they could not, they found a way they could. Over the course of 150 years, they have gone from the court steps to NASDAQ and we all have paid the cost.

Chapter 3
THE INVISIBLE MAN

"Oh, Br'er Rabbit, if we can't get it one way, we'll get it another."

~ American Folklore

This chapter could easily by written about the millions of men, women and children locked away in prison cells, targets of a racially biased system, removed not only from their families but their communities as well. They are a new class of people relegated to the back woods of small towns, forgotten by all but the children and families they left behind and the ones who now feed off their presence. It could be written about the millions of children who have grown into adulthood, seldom if ever having the benefit of their father or mother in their lives.[78] It could be written about families who go unnoticed, their poverty brought on by a parent taken from the home. It could be about the victim of drugs, addicts passed by on the street, invisible to the eye of many who choose not to see. It could be about those who sold the drugs when employment was not there or those who shot guns into unsuspecting crowds, vanishing before 911 was called. It could be about those who rob, break into cars and snatch purses when no one is around; their acts evidence of the desperation that erupt after years of racial oppression and failed attempts to find jobs in a market that makes no room. It could be about those whose spirit has been diminished by racism and hope extinguished by years of hate.

But this chapter, the most critical of all, is about the men and women who benefit from trafficking in human lives; those who multiply their profits lobbying Congress and state legislators who in turn convince an unsuspecting public that they are tough on crime. They rename the target of their perverse hatred and by someone else's standard, any consequence becomes justified. They label them criminals and few will oppose their fate. What were slave names in the old system are numbers in the new. At least slaves had a name, even if not their own.

This chapter is about those who garner billion of dollars each year to add more beds and build more prisons. They are the ones who convince Congress that no amount of billions is ever enough. This chapter is about those responsible for closed schools, closed mental institutions and reduced pay that keeps them rich. The ones who look for "candidates" to fill their prison beds. The invisible men and women are those who isolate themselves from the crowd and disconnect from the pain and destruction they cause. They are the few among us whose hearts have hardened and whose pockets are lined with the tears and blood of innocent children left behind. This chapter is about those behind the mask.

Who's Behind the Mask

Corrections Corporations of America

Corrections Corporation of America, is the largest commercial vendor of federal detainment and prisoner transport in the United States.[79] It is a private corporation founded in 1983, with headquarters in Nashville, Tennessee. It obtained its first contract in November of 1983, from the U.S. Department of Justice for The U.S. Immigration and Naturalization Service facility in Texas. The following year it assumed management of its first facility, a 63 bed juvenile facility in Shelby County, Tennessee. By April of that same year, CCA opened the Houston Processing Center. It was the first detention center in the world designed and constructed by a corrections company. For that they are proud. Within two years, CCA opened the Shelby Training Center in Shelby County, the first privately operated secure juvenile correctional facility in the United States. By October of that same year it went on the NASDAQ stock exchange at an initial share price of $9. At the time of this writing, its stock was trading on the New York Stock exchange at $34.52, down 1.40%.AX). When the headcount goes down, so does their stock. Their Commemorative 30th Anniversary Publication can be downloaded on-line. In 2013, CCA houses over 80,000 people in its 60 facilities. They own 44.

In addition to the profits earned through government contracts for prison acquisition, leasing and management, CCA also acquired CAI, Corrections Alternative, Inc, in August, 2013. CAI is a company that provides services for offenders, such as rehabilitation and education programs, substance abuse treatment, a specialized women's program, onsite Alcoholics Anonymous/Narcotics Anonymous meetings, life skills lessons, employment readiness, cultural diversity workshops, release planning and assistance in re-establishing family ties. In other words, after being complicit in destroying families and creating addictions to drug and alcohol as well as other dysfunctions through unjust and disparate mass incarcerations, CCA is also paid to provide services to undo the damage done.

Corrections Corporation of America functions with a board of 14 members. Its chairman is John Ferguson. Based on the biography listed for Ferguson, his life's work has been spent in building businesses and making money. There was no mention of volunteer or board service on any not-for profit corporations, though that is not to say that none exists. A Google search of John Ferguson, ironically brought up the execution of a mentally ill man by the same name in Florida. No other mention could be found other than his potential listing among the 25 other John Fergusons on LinkedIn, his inclusion in Forbes.com and reference to him in a PRNewswire.com article entitled "Former Commissioner of Finance and Administration For Tennessee, Named President and CEO of Prison Realty Trust, Inc. And Corrections Corporation of America".[80] According to the article, he was named president and CEO and then merged the troubled company with CCA to continue to buy and lease the real estate for the 60 prisons they own or manage. His focus appears to be making money, at all costs.

According to Forbes, in 2011, John Ferguson, earned a salary of $540,000, received "other compensation" in the amount of $72,583, non-equity incentive plan compensation of $1,080,000 and an additional $42,210 as a change in pension value and nonqualified deferred compensation earnings. His total compensation for 2011 was $1,734,793. His interest in managing the Immigration and Naturalization Services coupled with his million dollar incentive compensation could possibly be adding to the ongoing struggle for immigration reform. Fewer illegal immigrants would result in fewer beds filled.

More troubling when reviewing CCA's list of Board of Directors, is the presence of Thurgood Marshall Jr. As the son of the late U.S. Supreme Court Justice, Thurgood Marshall, a leader in securing many of the civil rights African Americans enjoy today, it is disturbing to see the name sullied by his active participation in an organization that profits from destroying so much of what his father fought to build. As stated in the book, *Thurgood Marshall, Justice for All*, his father was the U.S. Supreme Court's "...most eloquent spokesman for the rights of all Americans. He is the last of the justices from the Court of Chief Justice, Earl Warren who looked to the principles of the Bill of Rights and the Civil Rights amendments to protect the most powerless and despised among us."[81] To have worked so hard to protect the rights of the "powerless and despised" only to have his own son befoul such a stellar legacy is a tragedy in the annals of civil and human rights. A gifted lawyer, Thurgood Marshall Jr. no doubt justifies his presence on the board of CCA by arguments of the safety that prisons create. His argument would fail, however, in the face of facts. According to information shared during a 2012 Senate hearing on the exorbitant cost of incarcerations, the population of the federal prison system has increased exponentially over the exact same period of time that CCA has been in existence. Ironically, in 29 of the 30 years that CCA now celebrates, the incarceration of Americans in federal prisons has increased by nearly 800%.[82] No one is free of its grip.

While CCA heralds its 30 years of success, from the view of the average American, little has been accomplished. CCA has employed nearly 17,000 people to manage the 90,000 that they cage. That is 90,000 people who are depleting the tax base instead of building it up. That is 90,000 people who are not buying goods and services and 90,000 who do not contribute to their families' household budgets. CCA buys and leases the real estate it uses for the prisons it owns, managing to cut out anyone in the middle. And CCA partners with other corporations to create a complex system of wealth, but only for those at the top. While they boast of paying property and sales taxes in the communities in which they exist, they have removed far more from the communities in which their prisoners are taken. While they boast of having established a charitable fund from the billions they have reaped in profits, they have created billions of dollars of need in the communities across the United States. What CCA "gives back" is miniscule in comparison to what they gain.

Notwithstanding the human cost of incarcerations and the billions of dollars in direct costs, billions more are spent on the care and protection of children and families left behind. U.S. Hospitals annually assume hundreds of millions more in unpaid medical costs associated with domestic abuse and guns. The practice of incarcerating men and women for non-violent offenses in pursuit of higher stock prices rather than directing resources and business into their communities has devastated the lives of millions of children and, indeed, entire communities. According to a 2012, article, there has been nearly a 700% increase in immigrant detentions in private prisons in the last 30 years. Those three decades have a direct correlation to the formation of CCA. As part of the cumulative $45 million dollar lobbying investment of all private prison corporations, CCA shares in the largest portion of the return, $5.1 billion dollars in federal contracts.[83]

Crime and Punishment

In a period of one month in 2013, CCA lost four contracts in three states. According to reports, the contracts were terminated due to inhumane conditions, abuse, neglect, deaths, deadly riots, poor sanitation, prison gangs, inmate assaults and fraud.[84] And yet, even when fraud is discovered the only penalty suffered is the loss of a contract and potentially a government fine. Those who make their living detaining people who commit even the most minor crimes, will never themselves be imprisoned for stealing millions.

UNICOR – The Federal Prison Industries

Few Americans are aware of the existence of UNICOR, or what was originally enacted as the Federal Penal Industries in 1934. Formed with the purported purpose of providing jobs and training for prison inmates, it is the most glaring example of involuntary slave labor. It is run by a board of six directors all of whom are appointed by the sitting President of the United States. Currently the board members are David D. Spears, Chairman who represents Agriculture, Donald R. Elliott, Vice Chairman, representing Industry, Audrey J. Roberts, Member, Frank Gale,

71

representing Labor, and Lee Lofthus, represents the Attorney General. There is currently one vacancy, which, when filled represents the Secretary of Defense.

Information regarding UNICOR is readily available through a number of different sources, including its own web-site. The web-site, however, is frequently unavailable. When functioning, the web-site provides the history of the organization, annual reports and a plethora of products and services. Though it attempts to mask its connection to incarcerations and is far more sophisticated than the 19th Century convict leasing system, the similarities abound. As noted by one researcher, "[i]n looking at the website, it is obvious that the creators were trying to remove the organization from an association with the penal system. The name of the organization is changed from Federal Penal Industries to solely FPI or Unicor. The colors used on the website are mild (mainly white and light blues and greens) to elicit a calming sense for the visitor. On the front page, there are pictures of the multiracial people smiling and engaging in innocuous activities, including a young white man sitting and pondering in the prison yard, while a watch tower is shown in the background. Initially, it is not obvious that FPI is creating products and using the services of inmates. The front page is filled with buzz terms that can appeal to any socially conscious American citizen, such as "Made in America", "Solar and Renewable Energy" and "Green Inside and Out." The tagline for the website is "We're changing lives". [85]

"What is particularly harmful about this website is that FPI seems to be making the claim that it is producing better citizens from the prison population. There is no mention of the other aspects of these inmates' lives aside from their work with FPI that is aimed only at filling customers' orders. The website appears to be nothing more than a tool to facilitate FPI business transactions. There is no accountability or transparency to the public for the practices within prison walls. The various drop bars lead only to images of FPI services or manufactured products, ordering instructions and smiling inmates."[86]

Indeed, this author attempted to gain insight into the benefits and success of this program by inquiring through the web-sites contact page. Though ample time has passed since asking for the number of former UNICOR "employees" who have been gainfully employed using the trades they learned, no response has been received. Despite ongoing federal oversight and legislation used to create this purportedly self-sustaining industry that feeds off the human labor of its prey, FPI apparently feels no obligation to respond to the citizens of this country whose tax dollars are involuntarily involved.

Quoting a report by the Progressive Labor Party in an article written for the Center for Research on Globalization, the writer noted that the "prison industry complex is one of the fastest-growing industries in the United States and its investors are on Wall Street."[87] "This multimillion-dollar industry has its own trade exhibitions, conventions, websites, and mail-order/Internet catalogs. It also has direct advertising campaigns, architecture companies, construction companies, investment houses on Wall Street, plumbing supply companies, food supply companies, armed security, and padded cells in a large variety of colors."[88] While this statement applies to the overall prison industry, the interrelationship of UNICOR makes many of the aforementioned facts true of it as well.

By federal law, every medically able person confined to a federal prison must work. Based on UNICOR's 2013, report to Congress, in 2011, there were approximately 14,000 inmates employed in 88 FPI factories, down from 15,907 employed in 2010 and 94 factories operated.[89] Their employees manufacture items such as furniture, clothing, electronics, vehicular and metal products, and provide such services as printing, data processing and laundry.[90] The majority of federal prisoners work as plumbers, painters, food workers or groundkeepers. They earn as little as an astonishing 12¢ an hour. At best their pay can increase to a maximum of 28¢. As an alternative to working in maintenance for 40¢ or less an hour, approximately 16% of those incarcerated in federal prisons are lured into Federal Prison Industries (FPI) where factory wages start at 23¢ and increase to $1.15 an hour. Although the industry touts itself as providing workers marketable skills working in factory operations such as metals, furniture, electronics, textiles, and graphic arts, it disregards a job market with unemployment rates as high as 20%. Additionally, those trade jobs were traditionally controlled by unions and particularly at the time the law was enacted, Blacks were, for all intents and purposes, foreclosed from securing them. Even white who compete with others with no criminal background makes having a skill almost meaningless.

In addition to the hourly compensation many consider "slave wages", the Inmate Financial Responsibility Program

(IFRP) requires inmates to use 50% of their earnings to satisfy court-ordered fines, victim restitution, child support, and other monetary judgments. Some are required to pay Cost of Incarceration Fees.[91] Such requirements closely mirror those of the convict leasing system that captured even innocent men and women in the late 1800s and forced them to pay fines, restitution and fees.[92] Inability to pay meant forced work under those who had previously owned slaves. Further guaranteeing the full exploitation of those entangled in this system of duplicity and greed, for years, federal laws and regulations originally mandated that all federal agencies except the Department of Defense, purchase the products offered by UNICOR. Responding to the pressure of private industry, in 2004, Section 637 of Public Law 108-447 was enacted to change the mandatory requirement and open the door for competitive pricing. Still, in an industry where the largest provider pays more than $6.00 less an hour than the lowest paid job in private industry, competitive pricing is nearly impossible to achieve. In 2012, UNICOR was under fire for dominating its competitors with cheap prison labor, complaining that factories were at risk of closing and laying off employees.[93] In fact, both Alabama and Mississippi attribute factory closings and thousands of job losses to government contracts shifted to UNICOR.[94] Fueled by the threat of other closings, the Federal Prison Industries Competition in Contracting Act of 2013, was introduced in Congress by Republican Representative from Michigan, Bill Huizenga.[95] Supported by 15 co-sponsors, the bill attempts to curtail the struggle of private companies competing with the government run corporation that provides its workers no benefits and pays wages well below the otherwise minimum standard.[96] Despite such wages, however, UNICOR has managed to report a loss in its 2013 report to Congress. Though it was created to be self-sustaining, when friends and colleagues dip into the well, profits will disappear. Regardless of the loss felt by the government, profits were still earned by some.

GEO

The GEO Group, Inc. is a private corrections, detention and mental health treatment provider that maintains facilities in North America, Australia, South Africa and the United Kingdom. It was founded in 1984, by its current CEO, George Zoley, and is based in Boca Raton, FL. At the time of this writing, it was trading on the New York Stock Exchange as GEO, at 33.61. Its stock price was up 12%.

GEO employs 17,000 people to provide facility management, facility operation, facility maintenance, facility design, infrastructure financing, construction management, adult inmate management, secure prisoner escort, pre-trial and immigration custody services and community-based residential and re-entry services for its 73,000 beds in 93 detention and residential treatment facilities. The corporation is run by a six member board, George C. Zoley, Chairman of the Board, Chief Executive Officer and Founder, Richard H. Glanton, Chairman, CEO and Founder Philadelphia Television Network, Norman A. Carlson, Former Director, Federal Bureau of Prisons, Anne Newman Foreman Former Under Secretary, United States Air Force, Clarence E. Anthony, President and CEO of Anthony Government Solutions, Inc., Christopher C.

Wheeler, Former Member and Partner of Proskauer Rose LLP (Florida Office).

Originally founded in 1954, as Wackenhut Corrections Corporation (WCC), a division of The Wackenhut Corporation (TWC), in 1984, GEO founder, George C. Zoley became instrumental in the development and marketing of detention and correctional services to government agencies. Apparently competition from the Corrections Corporation of America, delayed it from acquiring its first contract for three years. In 1987, the federal government awarded GEO the Aurora Processing Center contract to provide secure care, custody, and control of 150 immigration detainees. After expanding into international markets, in 1993, it opened the world's largest in-prison therapeutic community chemical dependency treatment programs at the Kyle Correctional Center in Texas. The program provided intensive chemical dependency treatment. The following year it went public with an Initial Public Offering of 2.2 million shares on the NASDAQ® followed by a second offering in 1996, on the New York Stock Exchange. Between 1997 and 1998, concurrent with the federal government announcing mental health treatment facility closings across the country due to budget cuts, the company entered the area of residential treatment services to provide behavioral and mental health care services to state and local government agencies. During this period they received a contract award from the Federal Bureau of Prisons for the first privately operated facility, the Taft Correctional Institution as well as an award to operate and manage the first comprehensive privately-operated state psychiatric hospital in the US. In 1998, after forming a design company, GEO became the first private corrections company to have an in-house design team. In addition to a number of other services and acquisitions, in 2010, GEO acquired the Cornell Companies resulting in a growth of annual revenues of $1.5 billion dollars.[97] It has contracts with the Federal Bureau of Prisons, the U.S. Marshals Service, the U.S. Immigration and Customs Enforcement, eleven state correctional clients and various county and city jurisdictions to garner more than $134 million dollars in annual profits.

Despite being the second largest private corrections corporation in the United States, Zoley's compensation far exceeds that of his competitor. According to a report by PR Watch by The Center for Media and Democracy, which culled SEC records, Zoley has earned $22,315,704, in the four years between 2008 and 2012. Not his corporation, him. Most of his earnings are from taxpayer dollars.[98]

Though the news media never reports on the crimes that take place in prison, according to a report hundreds of lawsuits have been filed against it ranging from wrongful imprisonment to assault, rape, and even death.[99] The sizeable profits garnered by the GEO Group not only comes at the expense of those incarcerated but at the expense of its employees as well. According to the above referenced article, cost-cutting strategies have led to lower wages and benefits for workers, high employee turnover, insufficient training and under-staffing. It has increased violence, and riots, decreased medical care, and resulted in inadequate nutrition.[100] Industry wide there has been a 49% increase in attacks on guards.[101] A study by the U.S. Department of

Justice revealed that nationwide privately operated prisons experienced 65% more assaults against those incarcerated, and had significantly more escapes, homicides, and drug abuse compared to government-run prisons. [102] Interestingly, although more than a decade has passed since that 2001 study, apparently there is no interest in assessing more current data. No other government run study is available on-line. In 2013, the State of Mississippi terminated its contract with GEO "after it was found guilty of turning a juvenile facility into "a cesspool of unconstitutional and inhuman acts."[103] No criminal charges are mentioned.

It is important to understand that every prison, whether private or state run, generates billions of dollars in profits for those who build or maintain them. Private prisons however, are motivated to significantly increase the number of people confined and reduce costs for confining them. From the taxpayer, to the staff, to the overburdened families, to those who are incarcerated under extreme conditions, it seems apparent that few benefit from privately run prisons other than those who are making the profit and the legislators who accept the bribes.

ALEC

ALEC, the acronym for The American Legislative Exchange Council is a conservative action group that serves to advance the interest of some of the largest and wealthiest companies in the country. Among those companies are Koch Industries, Exxon Mobile and AT&T. Through the efforts of

Illinois Democratic U.S. Senator Richard Durbin, a highly protected list of some of its corporate members have been made available and are listed in the Incarcerations in Black and White Manual. Almost as if admitting to being a subversive organization, the ALEC web-site lists none of its members' names other than the board of directors. It also took exception to Senator Durbin having scouted out and published the information. According to the group Common Cause, ALEC has over 2000 legislative and corporate members who collaborate to secure laws that will advance their personal careers and corporate interests ahead of ordinary Americans.[104] In a PBS documentary hosted by acclaimed journalist, Bill Moyers, ALEC is referred to as "a vast network of corporate lobbying and political action aimed to increase corporate profits at public expense without public knowledge."[105] The introduction goes on to reveal through the use of interviews, documents and field reporting, that in "state houses around the country, hundreds of pieces of boilerplate ALEC legislation are proposed or enacted that would, among other things, dilute collective bargaining rights, make it harder for some Americans to vote, and limit corporate liability for harm caused to consumers — each accomplished without the public ever knowing who's behind it."[106]

In April 2012, the organization, Common Cause, filed an IRS whistleblower complaint alleging that ALEC misuses charity laws, massively underreports lobbying, and obtains improper tax breaks for corporate funders at the taxpayers' expense. The complaint was accompanied by 4000 ALEC documents submitted as evidence with supplemental documents filed in July of 2013.[107]

Though none of the private prison corporations appear on the list of known corporate members, according to the Center for Media and Democracy's PR Watch article, the GEO Group participated on an ALEC task force. ALEC is listed in this chapter on The Invisible Man because of its clandestine efforts that circumvent the best interest of U.S. citizens, including those that advance the interest of companies profiting from incarcerations. As stated on the ALEC web-site, "One of ALEC's greatest strengths is the public-private partnership. ALEC provides the private sector with an unparalleled opportunity to have its voice heard, and its perspective appreciated, by the legislative members."[108] Influence peddling at its best.

Incarcerations in Black and White

Chapter 4
DOUBLE VISION

"Judge not lest ye be judged."

~ *Matthew 7:1*

Today, double standards and volumes of laws continue to restrict the freedom of millions of American citizens, African Americans, immigrants, and other minorities in particular, while leaving in tack the privileges enjoyed by others. Black behavior itself is targeted and criminalized just as it was during the days of convict leasing and peonage.[109] Pretexts are used to deny rights that are otherwise clear. Prisons are filled with African Americans who engaged in behaviors routinely ignored when engaged in by whites. Not, as pointed out in *Slavery by Another Name*, "for any goal of enforcement or public protection against serious offenses, but purely to generate fees..."[110]

It is with the back drop of slavery, convict leasing and peonage, that we have to examine the current state of criminal affairs, the implications of that which makes one person's behavior criminal and, therefore, deserving of incarceration, and another's behavior, equally or even more debase in deed and intent, ignored, acceptable and often even praised. If we examine the so-called crimes of those currently locked in government run prisons, reduced to the status of animals and treated with disdain, it is obvious that most were for minor, non-violent offenses. They were literally coffled and corralled within concrete cages during the so-called War on Drugs, in the same manner slaves were shackled two centuries before. While their accusers sat in stately smoking rooms gulping glasses of aged bourbon and other legalized drugs, millions were labeled criminals for mollifying the pain of their bane existence with mere ounces of marijuana. One drug legal simply because someone deemed it to be so, the other illegal by the same stroke of the pen. One year liquor is illegal, the next it is not.[111] Today, men and women crowd prison cells trying to survive while corporate marauders toast each other's success in plundering billions from even the poor. Social deviance is determined not by any true moral standards but by those who measure with a yard stick that which privilege allowed them to draw.

Despite the existence of glaring inequities within the criminal justice system such as the gross disparities in sentencing guidelines, disproportionate representation of African Americans and the high rates of abused women and children, no disputation has convinced legislators to ameliorate the injustice that exists. After several years of effort, even influential U.S. Senators were unable to rally support for a bill that would have brought some degree of relief.[112] Although unanimously supported by the House of Representatives and co-sponsored by nearly 40 senators, Senate Republicans blocked a 2010 prison reform bill.[113] With the original sponsor no longer in the Senate, Senator Richard Durbin of Illinois is trying once again. The Smarter Sentencing Act was introduce in July of 2013, and is co-sponsored by Senators Patrick Leahy and Mike Lee.[114] It has a slim prognosis of actually being enacted.[115]

Pants on the Ground

A classic example of the double standards faced by African Americans is the response to the current trend of 'sagging", the style of dress allowing pants to hang well below the waistline thus exposing a portion of a person's covered derriere. While many towns across America give serious consideration to outlawing the much derided trend, several municipalities have already enacted laws making the fashion statement a crime. Pine Lawn, Missouri, a small, now predominantly African American municipality situated on the northwest boundary of St. Louis, was one of the first to make "sagging, illegal. The city ordinance calls for a monetary fine and community service for a second offense. Similar laws have also sprouted up, some include jail. Not only is potential jail time an egregious punishment for someone's choice of clothing, the very restriction that targets a style of dress indigenous to African American males is telling of a larger problem. These laws, like so many enacted since Reconstruction, are based, not on a behavior that threatens public safety, but on a manner of dress that deviates from what some consider to be the accepted style. The premise being that such attire "offends their sensibilities". Indeed, such restrictive laws have existed in the past. In a different time and different century, laws that restricted certain attire were aligned with a more Puritan society that opposed scant bathing suits or even skirts that rose above the ankle. There were Blue laws that restricted the sale of liquor on Sundays and others that restricted the general hours of operation. But in the 21st Century, laws in the United States had long evolved beyond the Puritan views of a few. Despite the repugnance of the current style of

85

sagging, it pales in comparison to the shirtless and barefoot hippies who blanketed public parks, sidewalks and establishments across the country during the 60s. Sagging pants show far less than white men who mow their lawns or grace public parks in nothing more than shorts- hairy chests and inflated bellies in full view. The low riding pants that cut across the midsection of a young man's buttocks, often exposing designer shorts, do not hold a candle to the countless overweight plumbers who have bent over in kitchens across America exposing far more than any human eye should see. Despite such impropriety, not only was this form of attire not outlawed but the term "plumber's crack" made its way into the American lexicon. Many an African American male would have been arrested on the grounds of exposing himself to the homeowner's gentile wife. Even worse, history has shown he would have been convicted and served time.

What is even more disturbing about outlawing a dress style indigenous to African American men is the acceptance of a white man standing in the middle of Time Square playing a guitar in nothing more than underwear. For 15 years, the City of New York has not only allowed a half-naked man to stand in the midst of men, women and children in one of the most visited tourist attractions in the entire world, but eventually even granted its blessing. This man, dubbed "The Naked Cowboy" has franchised the duplication of his personalized exposure and has sued successfully in State Court for franchise infringement. The very legal system that deems unlawful an African American man's right to wear his attire in a manner he deems fit, protects the right of a white man to do just the same.[116]

While Black boys and men alike are hyper policed, stopped, frisked and detained for no reason other than looking like a purported suspect that matches their description, white males are free to drive, walk or run where they chose. Indeed, the U.S. Supreme Court case of Illinois v Wardlow,[117] has legalized the suspicion and, therefore, search of an individual for running when seeing a law enforcement officer. Like other laws that result in the disparate representation of African Americans in the criminal justice system, there is a strong probability that the Court's sanction is being discriminately used most often, if not exclusively, on African Americans or other minorities where hyper policing already takes place. Like the language used in the "crack" legislation, the case serves as a pretext for targeting, chasing and frisking Blacks. That conclusion is supported by empirical data that shows that Blacks are stopped, searched and arrested more frequently than whites under the pretext of traffic stops even though Blacks are no more likely to have weapons or drugs than whites.[118] Further, the hyper-policing of African American communities, the constant suspicion, unwarranted stops, harassment, framing and other negative consequences of encountering police for generations, is a factor that is as likely to result in an individual fleeing police as is an actual illegal act.

The truth of this reality became glaringly clear one summer day when walking past a downtown sports bar. At 11:30 a.m. on a school day one particular table was surrounded by six school age boys and two men. Each youngster, looking no more than 11 or 12, was clad in a bright, red shirt that bore the name of their favorite Cardinals player. With the excitement of baseball in the downtown air, it was obvious they were having an early lunch before heading to the game. One of their fathers made his way around the table making sure each boy was content. None of them were Black. This was a Thursday, not a Saturday or some national holiday that just happened to coincide with the Cardinals v Marlin game. This was a school day. Driving past the ball park just a few blocks away, the reserved prerogative was further played out. Bright red seats in the stadium had already begun to fill and outside more school aged boys headed for the gates. Father's walked along side and police parted the way.

This scene plays out daily throughout America. Fathers and sons ignore laws and protocol and head for the game. Superintendents and police chiefs alike turn their heads as thousands of school age boys (and a few girls I suppose) take off from school and attend afternoon games at the park. While thousands of fathers and sons stop for leisurely meals and ready themselves for a day of fun, African American boys and girls who similarly "play hooky" are detained and sent to detention centers. While parents of African American youth are penalized for their children's truancy, uniformed police escort the privileged class across the street. Thus goes justice in America.

It is our silence in the everyday disparities of justice that emboldens the dominant class and gives way to egregious laws. Unlike the choices of little Black boys and girls and all children of lesser means, this public disregard for state law is given a nod of the head. Life for minorities and impoverished whites in America is far different from their counterparts who can afford baseball tickets, official team shirts, and meals at Ozzie Smith's. Yet we remain silent when the same double standard is displayed before football games where tailgate parties routinely take place on parking lots and nearby streets. Large groups of men and women gather to down gallons of beer, blast music and cook 'dogs on open fires just inches from car tanks full of gas. Curse words and country music fill the downtown air while tourists and residents meander nearby. Not a ticket is issued or arrest made for disorderly conduct. No mention is made of vagrancy or concern expressed by city officials for the fire hazards that lurk near the exhaust pipes of nearly every parked car.

Contrary to these scenes, such deference was not shown toward young Black men who gathered on street corners, singing four part harmony and telling tales. Some drank from brown paper bags and a few may have lit up. In colder months fires burned in trash cans to keep their hands warm - but none were close enough to gas tanks to ignite an entire city block. These men were harassed or even arrested for vagrancy and run from every corner in town. Their gatherings were deemed unlawful and seen as threats to city visitors, their singing deemed nuisance and their light hearted laughter a disturbance of the peace.

This is life in America. White privilege is white privilege. Whether it is complicity in mass truancy for little white boys or tailgate parties that all but hang signs for "Whites Only", the unwritten rules are not much different today than in 1960. White men can traverse city parks with hairy chests and bulging bellies while African American boys are arrested for letting high priced briefs show above sagging pants. Theaters fill public venues with vulgarity from three New Jersey boys while municipalities restructure streets and parking signs to deter Blacks who cruise and blast their music. "They" can take off a day from work to attend a baseball game while many African Americans are fired for showing up 10 minutes late.

The message sent to whites and Blacks alike is that rules and privileges are simply not the same. Though sagging pants are less than a desirable style for most and playing hooky whether condoned or not is wrong, the greater tragedy in these facts is the blatant and unfair disparity in the response to African American behavior. Since the enactment of the 13th Amendment laws, policies and unwritten rules have criminalized the conduct of African Americans. The freedom of African Americans to move and act in the same manner as whites is restricted and made illegal only because a majority of legislators have deemed it to be so. Seldom are those majorities Black. The "Whites Only" signs have disappeared from all but museums, but "Whites Only" rights have persisted to this day.

As we progress through the 21 Century, signs that say "no Blacks allowed" may not be seen but the end results are the same. While African American men increasingly fill prison cells and unemployment lines, little white boys will always be welcome in ball parks during the day and tailgaters still exercise their right to prevail. After all, in an America that only pretends to inclusive, it is still all about baseball, mom and apple pie and privilege is still reserved for just for "them". The double standard is apparent in the absence of the young Black men who kept vigil on street corner steps since the 60s doing nothing more than singing four part harmony and drinking beer from brown paper bags. They have all but disappeared. Police have either disbanded the groups or worse, they have all been targeted for jail. In the meantime, white males congregate in loud boisterous groups in parking lots and side streets at every major game. Name them "tailgate parties" and no degree of profanity, loud music, excessive drinking or even fires burning just inches from gas tanks elicits even the slightest attention from police. While young Black boys are locked up for truancy when "playing hooky", young white boys are escorted to noontime baseball games with policemen escorting them across the street. While Black men are stopped for no more than driving while Black, white men turn over keys to their under aged sons. While Black boys are locked in detention when curfew is broken, white boys are escorted home.

The contradiction of these examples illuminate the hypocrisy and injustice that continues to permeate our society. The criminalization of a dress code that has no correlation to crime or public safety, (other than its origin being attributed to prisons where belts are not allowed) while sanctioning a far greater public display of exposure by a person of privilege, is a glaring example of racial impetus in lawmaking.

To move toward a less punitive society, one intolerant of racial injustice, it is necessary to properly frame the lawmaking process in its true light. We have been taught to readily accept the concepts of "illegal" and "criminal" as that which has been enacted into law without adequately questioning the process and reasoning behind them. Notwithstanding the formidable efforts to create a system of checks and balances, history has proven that ideals written into governing documents do not guarantee perfection in execution.

What is and is not deemed illegal in the United States, whether on the federal, state or municipal level, is not determined by an omniscient power. Laws that determine the legality or illegality of our choices are not enacted by entities maintaining neutral stances towards all, but are created by fallible human beings whose self-interest, prejudices, outside pressures and hardened hearts have far more influence on the decision making process than does a sense of justice and fair play. One need look back only a few years, if not at more arcane laws of today, to site a plethora of laws replete with unjust measures and weights.

California's three strikes law that impacts minorities in greatly disproportionate numbers, as well as those related to the so called War on Drugs, are among those most disturbing. Few are unaware of the grossly unfair sentencing guidelines that put tens of thousands of African American's behind bars for use or possession of crack cocaine while their white counter parts, it prosecuted at all, were given sentences far less punitive.

Behavior becomes illegal merely by the decisions of those the electorate puts in power. When the majority of the populace is guided by racist beliefs, those they elect to office will prove their worthiness to hold office by crafting laws that reflect their constituents' beliefs. Even worse, is the so called system of checks and balances, the Executive, the Judiciary and the Legislative branches of government, traditionally have been filled by individuals sharing the same limited view. The U.S. Supreme Court upheld miscegenation laws for decades, making it illegal for Blacks and whites to intermarry. It was not until 1967 that the court made such laws as Virginia's Racial Integrity Act of 1924 invalid in the case of Loving v Virginia.[119] The same is true of laws that upheld segregation, discrimination in employment, and even the murder of slaves. All "legal" conduct simply because it was deemed so by a group of all white males. It is the inverse of those legalities, repugnant to the moral sense of some, that direct law makers to deem illegal that which simply impugns the choices of others.

Despite alcohol being attributed to more than 11,000 fatal accidents a year and a causal factor in domestic violence and numerous other violent crimes; despite it impairing judgment and affecting the brain's performance, the manufacture, sell, purchase, possession and use of alcohol remains legal, while marijuana, has been a primary factor in the arrests, convictions and incarcerations of millions of men and women since the Sixties. Just as the illegalization of opium in the late 1800s, the choice of drug used by many Chinese immigrants who had been both unwanted and barred from entry into the United States, was used to imprison thousands of Chinese and destroy their highly successful businesses,[120] the possession, sale and even use of marijuana has been used to destroy African American neighborhoods and fill prison beds. Poor whites and Hispanics likewise used to increase prison profits.

There are countless examples of unjust treatment that date back for decades. The theft of a ham to feed a family of hungry children warrants several years in prison,[121] while corporate bosses "steal" billions of dollars from the masses and remain free. As stated by one NBC journalist, "mortgage borrower got targeted, bankers got billions."[122] While federal officials decline prosecuting mortgage lenders and bankers for fraud, predatory practices and other illegal actions that plummeted an entire world economy into chaos, the NBC story revealed that IRS agent, Robert Nordlander, targeted a man who had run 4600 miles in the Sahara desert to raise money for clean water projects in Africa. The agent spent over 700 hours investigating how the runner managed to train for and run such a distance while also maintaining a full time job.[123] After being convicted for exaggerating his income on a mortgage application (as thousands of lenders encouraged), the runner spent a year and a half in federal prison away from his two teenage sons. Courts have ruled that burning a baby to death with saline solution in utero is deemed legal but choking one to death seconds after its birth is not.[124] Building sub-standard housing that results in the deaths of dozens is excused, while accidentally killing someone in a normal exchange of blows is not. Writing a check without funds in the bank is illegal but banks stealing billions of dollars from its customers through manipulation of fees is not.[125] Black students engaged in fights are suspended from school while white students are sent back to class. The number of such randomly written and enforced laws goes well beyond enumeration.

Prisons are overrun with millions of African American men and women not because African Americans are more innately criminal but because laws are created and enforced targeting their behaviors. Thefts, drug use, assault and even murders that do, in fact, occur in African American communities, are brought about not because African Americans are hardwired to steal, abuse drugs, fight or murder but because conditions in an increasingly oppressive country create circumstances where thefts rather than jobs are, for many, the only realistic means of survival. Drug abuse becomes the norm when rejection, oppression, inability to support one's family, and other social ills become more than an individual can bear. And, with most murders occurring through the use of firearms, one must question the source of such weapons. Few, if any, gun manufacturing plants are owned by an African American. Few if any drug manufacturers are Black and few own the planes and boats to transport loads of illegal drugs from other countries. Blacks, therefore are merely the low hanging fruit; more easily targeted and more often convicted.

Now as then, when drug use on the streets of Black ghettos was more prevalent than hope, drugs are still being filtered into Black neighborhoods. Heroin, originally invented and freely distributed by the Bayer Drug Company, is once again on the rise. With jobless rates in double digits, its sell is alluring to many unemployed and marginalized men and women who seek financial refuge to support themselves and their families. With despair, discrimination and social deviance a daily reality in many African American neighborhoods, they are often more willing to engage in its use.

The Failed War on Drugs

Although the War on Drugs has been often referred to as a failure,[126] an evaluation of the billions of dollars spent to lock up drug users and traffickers, while making not a dent in the trade, The War on Drugs was, in fact, a glaring success. For those who designed this civil attack against its own citizens, The War on Drugs did exactly what it was supposed to do, funnel billions of dollars into the upper echelons of the drug world, assure the death or disability of millions of African American men, women and children who died or became its human carnage, imprisoned millions more so called drug offenders, assured billions were made through the construction and maintenance of prisons and guaranteed the election of thousands of politicians who won office and countless gifts. They instilled fear in the minds of the voters and chalked up another win. Ultimately it was the intentional addiction of African Americans that measured the War's success.

Often when the words "billions were spent" or "billions were wasted" are used, images are conjured up of our hard earned dollars being flushed down a drain or going up in smoke. In fact, the trillions spent to bailout morally corrupt bankers, the trillions spent on the War on Drugs and the trillions of dollars spent to build and maintain prisons have been spent exactly as intended. They lined the pockets of the nation's wealthy and added a few more millionaires to the rolls. The expenditures of tax payer funds has done little for the rest of society, even those who wish to identify with the rich. It has done little more than create empty dreams chased by those doing the work of two, taking home the pay of one. Those caught in this mirage of success find themselves neglecting families while catering to more wealth or themselves breaking laws that lead them to jail. While mansions once reserved for Hollywood's best are now staples in neighborhoods across America, there is still a clamor of discontent. There is a constant quest for more while looking down on others, grabbing for elusive stars and using human beings as a means to an end that will never be enough. The more America disdains another people, the more it seeks to wreck the lives of minorities and the less fortunate the more havoc will be reeked on all. The consequences of sin are death. And death is on the rise.

Chapter 5

IT'S JUST GEOGRAPHY

"We will never have true civilization until we have learned to recognize the rights of others."

~ *Will Rogers*

One of the greatest indications that the label "criminal" strips an individual of humanity, is the statistical reporting of crime itself. No sooner than crime reports are released by the Department of Justice, than lists of the most dangerous cities in America are compiled. The lists, however, consistently ignore two very significant factors, white collar crime that occurs with much greater frequency than those reported and crimes that occur within prison walls.

Needless to say, when you take a group of people convicted of crimes, remove them from the only sense of security and support they know, corral them inside concrete walls and cage them in cells or massive dorms then treat them like animals, it is likely that violence will result. Every day young boys convicted of no more than possession of marijuana are raped, men are slashed with crude weapons honed from the most unlikely objects, gladiator fights are arranged by prison guards and gang violence is the norm. When it comes to crimes behind bars, creativity knows no limit. Inmates are beaten, property stolen, even criminal drug rings are run from the very walls that imprison them. Despite all the crime that takes place behind prison doors, when crime statistics are gathered those crimes are ignored. As though a conviction renders a person ineligible for concern, the brutal slashings, beatings and rapes,[127] many by the correctional staff itself,[128] are omitted from the final count.

Those who crunch the numbers, more accurately those that request they be crunched, elect to focus only on crimes that generate fear. The fear mongering that gets politicians elected and budget increases passed requires that only the crime next door is seen. They direct focus on home robberies while lenders steal the house. The far more pervasive crime that takes place in corporate boardrooms result in billions in bank fees stolen from customers, billions in homes foreclosed and billions in tax dollars diverted to padded bills. But they are seldom referred to as crimes; never listed on the charts. The white collar crimes that plummet 401(k)s and steal from workers to fund CEO's checks, by choice do not make the list. The lists that tell of crime in America deceptively place full onus on crimes on the street. They drive conversations in classrooms, steer academic research, provide fodder for books and create fear in an unsuspecting public. Those lists, however, consistently fail to mention the unseen crimes of corporate criminals and protect them in their ruse.

But even the crimes that make the list do not cease simply because those who commit them are moved behind prison walls. Their temporary absence has not made the community safer. Indeed, the astronomical increase in incarcerations themselves, presumably for crimes committed, would suggest that prisons make the community less safe, not more.

As former President George Bush noted in his State of the Union address in 2004, "This year, some 600,000 inmates will be released from prison back into society. We know from long experience that if they can't find work, or a home, or help, they are much more likely to commit more crimes and return to prison... America is the land of the second chance, and when the gates of the prison open, the path ahead should lead to a better life."[129] Seldom does that path exist. Studies show that within three years of release two-thirds of those individuals will return to prison.[130] However, in 2007, with budget challenges that faced every other state, the State of Texas invested $241 million into evidenced-based strategies to reduce recidivism. Since those reforms went into effect, Texas has saved almost $2 billion in new prison spending. Additionally, the parole failure rate is down 39 percent and the statewide crime rate is down to levels not seen since the 1960s, a time predating the push towards prisons for profits.[131]

It has been known for decades that a person entering prison for a minor, non-violent offense will return to society with an advanced degree in crime. Rather than list statistics to substantiate this fact, it may be more convincing if you, as the reader simply look at your own life. Those who lived through the 1960s and 1970s, though affected by the tragic events of the Vietnam War, the war protests, campus riots and the assassination of Medgar Evers, John F. Kennedy, Malcolm X, Dr. Martin Luther King Jr., and Robert Kennedy, may also remember the tranquility of their personal lives. Few from that era will ever forget the race riots or the unassailable pain of segregation and discrimination. But in their own lives, many were able to carve out a degree of safety and normalcy. In many neighborhoods the door to your home could be left unlocked. Children ran in and out slamming screen doors. Open windows welcomed cool breezes day and night. Bicycles and toys cluttered front yards, left unattended until their owners reclaimed their use. Car windows were left down, rolled up only at the threat of rain. The only alarm needed to warn of an unlikely intruder was the family dog. Clothing and rugs hung safely on backyard lines, deliveries were left at the door. You could walk into any bank and cash any check and into schools that had no guards. Lockers were left unlocked and children walked home safely from school. Kidnappings happened only to the rich and drugs only to a few. Guns were the exception rather than the rule, the NRA had not yet scared the masses. Church doors remained unlocked all nights and prayers were prayed in schools. You could sit on your porch or lay under the stars. On hot summer nights, some slept in public parks. Drive by shootings were unheard of and children stayed out until the street lights came on. There was no credit card fraud and no one hacked your account (though the internet was still unknown.)

As time progressed, there were reminders that things had changed. Car doors were routinely locked and valuables were tucked away. Windows were rolled up rain or shine. Purses that had rested on seats were suddenly put on the floor. Doors were locked at night and eventually at all times; dead bolts were added, then bars and alarms. Rather than hang out clothes to dry, driers or Laundromats became an added expense. As drive-bys increased, porches emptied out. Couples stopped taking evening strolls and few went out at night. The elderly could no longer rock on their porches watching children play. They no longer sipped ice water and basked in the summer breeze. Many died from fires, others from sweltering heat; locked behind windows that were locked and barred. Times have changed and not always for the better. Decades after the prison profligate began, no one is immune from crime. While it appears that crime is more prevalent in inner city burgs, those committed by whites either go unreported or simply seldom pursued. While some move away from inner city crime, they take with them self-inflicted bars. Fear confines them to their communities and block out much of what goes on outside. They, too must lock their doors and program alarms. They too have been murdered, bludgeoned and raped. Despite the unprecedented use of prisons to purportedly keep us safe, society is far less safe today than ever before; certainly less free.

In reality, any method used to deter crime that fails to recognize the humanity of every human being does nothing more than shift crime from one segment of society to another. That is just geography. Indeed, it has been acknowledged that the decrease in drug dealing in one neighborhood as a result of successful police techniques, did nothing more than shift the drug dealing from one part of town to another.[132] Though drug addiction and the safety of the overall community should be the concern, greater emphasis is placed on removing drugs from a specific area than on eliminating the trade overall.

Despite data to the contrary, politicians paint deceptive pictures and win votes with promises of being tough on crime. But once in office they succumb to the demands of lobbyists and enact laws that put us all at greater risk. Legislators enact more laws and approve more prisons while closing their eyes to the children left behind and ignoring the pleas educators' make for funding. They feign concern for victims of crime but take actions that increase the risks. The smoke and mirrors politicians used to convince voters of their purported success, conceal the reality of everyday life. With more than 650,000 men and women being released from prison every year (10,000 each week),[133] it is only so long before the smoke disappears and the image in the cracked mirror appears more real. When the reality of limited jobs obstruct successful re-entry, many of those released will return to prison and leave a trail of victims in their path. Like the mortgage debacle that fell like a house of cards, there will always be a straw that breaks the camel's back.

Consider the case of Oklahoma, a state synonymous with many things. There is the great musical by the same name with actors clad in western garb singing and dancing with glee. There are the deer and buffalo roaming free on the range, until that is, they are shot and their heads mounted on walls. There is the Oklahoma City bombing, one of those tragic events that can be marked by knowing exactly where you were when the news was first heard. There are the names Timothy McVey and Terry Nichols, forever etched in our collective minds as the boys next door who killed 111 men, women and children. And then there are the tornadoes.

Oklahoma. There, just north of Texas and leaning toward the westward expansion, a state known for its resiliency behind one tragedy after another. Oklahoma has another claim to fame; one in which, understandably it rarely ever boasts, at least not outside of a convention of Corrections Corporations of America or in the halls of the Republican National Convention. Oklahoma holds the title, proudly or otherwise, of being the leading state in America in incarcerating women. With 4,826 women incarcerated, Oklahoma tops even Texas in raw numbers. As if racing to the top echelon of an esteemed chart, Oklahoma is rapidly increasing the incarceration of even mothers.[134] One mother's prison sentence of 12 years for selling $31 worth of marijuana exemplifies the aberrant use of prisons and reckless disregard for the overall impact on children and society. Once portrayed as a wholesome Western state where "never was heard a discouraging word", Oklahoma's record of incarceration is enough to make women across America rethink entering their borders and for America to be seen in a light other than "Mom and apple pie". Clearly something much more insidious is baking in the boardrooms of one of America's more iconic states. And the best interest of its women and children are no longer a part of the recipe.

Worse than the transitive trend of incarcerating women, is the collateral consequence of incarcerating mothers, those women who are too often a child's sole provider. In a fifteen year period between 1997 and 2012, Congress and state legislatures have allowed a staggering 122% increase in the incarceration of mothers.[135] Those women leave behind thousands of children, often to fend for themselves or to be torn apart in a foster care system that may ultimately terminate the mother's parental rights. In too many instances, the woman's introduction to conduct deemed illegal evolved from a spouse or significant other being imprisoned. With one parent gone and no longer able to contribute to an already diminished household income, alternatives are sought to survive. Many turn to prostitution simply to pay their bills. They are arrested, charged and imprisoned for trying to support their children the only way they know how. When a spouse is incarcerated, the mother is also left with the emotional pain of the separation, the stress of witnessing the impact on their children, the demands of replacing a lost income and often making new school and living arrangements. Some in turn are driven to seek solace in criminalized drug usage as well as to petty theft in order to support their habits. The circle of incarceration in one family then becomes complete, both mother and father removed from the home and children unceremoniously added to an already over-burdened foster care system.

To further exacerbate the injustice and insensitivity toward the plight of our fellow human beings, according to a report by the Center for American Progress, 85 to 90% of all women who have been incarcerated were victims of abuse.[136] Acknowledging that "sexual violence, drug dependence, and poverty are all strongly correlated with women's incarceration", the report's author notes that our society still "chooses to punish instead of heal—we lock women up instead of providing services that could help them live healthy, secure, and productive lives."[137] But those numbers make perfect sense from the perspective of those who profit and influence legislators. For 12 out of 13 years, the Oklahoma Department of Corrections sought emergency funds from the state Legislature. Using the approach to imprison rather than heal, the prison population grew from 17,983 inmates in 1995 to 26,720 in 2010. State appropriations increased from $188 million to more than $461 million.[138] The amount requested for 2014, is $592 million. While the Department of Corrections Director, Justin Jones, begged the Oklahoma state legislature for a $6.4 million supplemental appropriation at a January, 2013, hearing, the 2014 state budget left the Department of

Education more than $200 million dollars below their 2008, budget.[139] Needless to say, inflation makes those figure even more difficult to stretch.

To get a sense of the how much money is being spent on those in our society who would be much better served by treatment, alternate sentencing programs, elimination of racial oppression, fairness in contract allocation, job creation, balanced allocation of corporate profits and just plain human decency, following is the 2014 Allocation Request for the Oklahoma Department of Corrections.

Summary

Oklahoma Department of Corrections
FY 2014 Appropriation Request

Priority	Item	See Page	Funding Existing Authorized FTE	Personnel Costs	Contract Services	Operating Costs	Total
A	Market Adjustment for Classified Employees	2		$12,200,000			$12,200,000
B	Funding for Staffing Adjustments	3	54.0	2,998,533			2,998,533
C	Offender Growth and Per Diem Restoration	4			$13,697,537	--	13,697,537
D	Operating Costs	5				$9,313,111	9,313,111
E	Non-Discretionary Increases – Medical Services	7			1,116,000	8,384,000	9,500,000
F	Non-Discretionary Increases – T&RS	10			50,000	1,232,850	1,282,850
G	Efficiency Improvements	13				634,000	634,000
H	Infrastructure and Equipment Improvements	14				9,197,730	9,197,730
I	Improvements to Maintain or Increase Security	17				6,331,100	6,331,100
J	Improvements to Maintain Vehicles	19				810,000	810,000
K	Information Technology/Other Technology Upgrades	20				749,000	749,000
	Total Requested Appropriation Increase		54.0	$15,198,533	$14,863,537	$36,651,791	$66,713,861
	FY 2013 Appropriation						$463,731,068
	TOTAL REQUESTED APPROPRIATION FOR FY 2014						$530,444,929

FY 2014 Budget Request Priority A

A. Item Description

Salary Increase for Classified Employees

B. Cost

5% Market Adjustment Increase for Classified Employees	$12,200,000

Non-competitive hiring rates are affecting the Department of Corrections' ability to recruit and retain employees who are responsible for providing public safety.

Adjust compensation of all classified employees by 5%.

Increase hiring rate for Correctional Officers from $11.83 / hour to $14.00 / hour.

Estimated number of classified employees affected - 3,565 FTE dispersed statewide.

Estimated cost is $12.2 million (inclusive of mandatory benefits).

Total - Classified Pay Raise   **$12,200,000**

C. Justification

These funds are needed to retain and recruit staff who are essential to ensuring public safety is not compromised.

Contact: Greg Sawyer, Chief of Departmental Services, 425-7290
Greg.sawyer@doc.state.ok.us

2

107

FY 2014 Budget Request Priority B

A. Item Description

Necessary staffing for added requirements resulting from HB 3052

B. Cost

<u>Community Corrections</u>

	FTE	
Probation and Parole Officers; Statewide HB 3052 (JRI)	45.0	$2,522,970
Probation and Parole Team Supervisors; HB 3052 (JRI)	5.0	334,715
Administrative Technicians III; HB 3052 (JRI)	4.0	140,848

Total - Needed to fund existing authorized FTE* **54.0** **$2,998,533**

C. Justification

These funds are necessary to meet operational requirements mandated in HB 3052.

*No new FTE authorizations are needed for this request. The request is only for funding to fill FTE positions that are currently vacant.

Contact: Greg Sawyer, Chief of Departmental Services, 425-7290
Greg.sawyer@doc.state.ok.us

3

108

FY 2014 Budget Request Priority C

A. Item Description
Offender net growth results in contract growth and per diem restoration.

B. Cost

Contracted Beds - Growth

Jail Backup
Additional funding needed for 1,400 bed average $1,413,507

Private Prison Beds
Jefferson County – Waurika
96 beds Oct. 1, 2012 $877,968
CCA-Cimarron Corr. Facility
240 beds July 1, 2012   3,857,028
CCA-Cimarron and Davis Corr. Facilities
100 beds Oct. 1, 2012   1,202,019

Additional funding for 436 beds added in FY 2013 $5,937,015

Annualizing the FY 2013 Supplemental
A supplemental appropriation was requested to increase
per diem rates for Private Prisons and Halfway Houses.
This request asks for the annualization of that appropriation
to continue the per diem increase requested in the
supplemental. $2,000,000

A supplemental appropriation was requested to address the
population growth the Agency is experiencing due to 85%
sentencing law and longer sentences. This request asks for
annualization of that appropriation to continue the funding
needed for added growth. $3,787,815

A supplemental appropriation was requested to support the
requirements of HB 3052 to provide "intensive
programmatic services". This request asks for
annualization of that appropriation less one-time costs for
facilitator training to continue the funding for programmatic
services. $559,200

Total – Contract Offender Growth   **$13,697,537**

C. Justification
Added growth will require resources necessary to maintain these
offenders.
Per diem restoration for private vendors will improve operating
capabilities.

Contact: Greg Sawyer, Chief of Departmental Services, 425-7290
Greg.sawyer@doc.state.ok.us

4

FY 2014 Budget Request Priority D

A. Item Description

Operating cost required for 2014 not budgeted in 2013:

B. Cost

Community Corrections	$600,000

Reoccurring cost due to HB 3052 mandate
Office space @10.00 sq. ft./150 sq. ft. per officer
Copy machine leasing @500.00 yr./per location
Phones, fax, DSL cost 1,000.00 yr./per location
Office supplies 3.70 per offender
Safety/drug test supplies 63.00 per officer

Agency-Wide

Utilities	$580,543
Food	832,996
Fuel	198,710
Offender Clothing	4,066,162
Correctional Officer Uniforms	851,200
Office Space Rent Increases	50,000
Bill Johnson Correctional Center Jail Pads and Mattresses	43,500

Operating costs required for 2014 that are not a part of the 2013 budget

Pharmaceutical Contract	$1,000,000

There are approximately 1,460 Certified Judgment and Sentence offenders awaiting transfer to ODOC from county jails. Due to the Attorney General's opinion 2011-19, ODOC is required to pay for medical care including prescriptions for those awaiting transfer. The Agency is also anticipating an increase in prescription costs associated with the Justice Reinvestment Act. Currently, the average prescription cost per offender is $39.03 per month. We are estimating the total annual cost increase to be $1,000,000.

Transfers (Third Party Payer)	$1,000,000

This increase represents payments to health care providers for non-routine care including medical specialty care, hospital admission and hospital emergency care. Offenders included in this category are approximately 1,460 Certified Judgment and Sentence offenders awaiting transfer to ODOC and those

Contact: Greg Sawyer, Chief of Departmental Services, 425-7290   5
Greg.sawyer@doc.state.ok.us

110

FY 2014 Budget Request Priority E

A. Item Description

  Non-Discretionary Increases – Medical Services

B. Cost

Medical Services
  Pharmaceutical Contract $616,000

  The Centers for Medicare and Medicaid (CMS) offer projections for
  health care expenditures. Long term projections have been
  generally reliable. The CMS Healthcare Fact Sheet has predicted a
  rise in pharmaceutical costs of 6.1%. That number has varied over
  recent years from 6.1 to 6.3%. The lower number was chosen as a
  more conservative estimate. These numbers reflect national
  spending trends. The onset of The Affordable Care Act will change
  this trend nationally, but will not necessarily change trending for
  ODOC. Additionally, the aging of the offender population is a
  significant factor connected to pharmaceutical costs. From 2008 to
  2012, the percentage of ODOC offenders who are greater than 50
  years of age rose from 14.3% to 17.1%. As the offender population
  ages, costs of age related pharmaceuticals will increase due to
  increased utilization by older offenders.

  Reimbursement to Private Prisons for HIV Medications $330,000

  Until early 2012, the cost of HIV medications had not been passed
  on to ODOC by all private prisons. Based upon the monthly
  reimbursement requests to date from one particular private prison
  alone, we are projecting an average annual increase of $255,000,
  not including anticipated price increases. As of August, 2012 ODOC
  lists 135 HIV positive offenders, 26 of which are at private prisons
  and 109 housed in ODOC facilities. This number of offenders is a
  relatively stable number for ODOC, ranging from about 130 to 150
  total HIV positive offenders. Newer combination medications are
  becoming available, which do gradually drive medication costs
  higher. As an example, expenditures for one such medication,
  Atripla, have risen over the past year from $64,633.00 to $99,138.00
  (a 53.4% increase). Over the past 12 months, total expenditures for
  HIV medications have risen by 22.9%. The average cost to treat an
  HIV offender is about $1,858 per month.

  Hepatitis C Drug Cost Increase $3,000,000

  The treatment of Hepatitis C is evolving in a manner similar to the
  evolution of HIV treatment in the 1990's. ODOC has partnered with
  the Nazih Zuhdi Transplant Institute and is conducting telehealth

111

Operating Costs (continued)

qualifying for the Justice Reinvestment Act. Typically, non-routine costs are about one-third the cost of total medical care, which equates to $1.94 not including pharmaceuticals. We are anticipating the total annual costs to be $1,000,000.

Joseph Harp CC Infirmary Space Expansion $90,000

The following items are needed to convert a portion of the J Unit at Joseph Harp CC to infirmary space. The renovation costs will be minimal due to existing space being American Disability Act compliant, and sufficient security cameras in place. Building renovations will only involve the purchase and installation of an observation/pill line window (48" x 72") and related supplies.

Electric Hospital Beds w/mattress and rails - 68 @ $1,100 ea.	$74,800
Scale to accommodate wheelchair – 1 @ $2,000 ea.	2,000
Vital Signs with BP/Pulse Ox/Temperature – 2 @ $1,200 ea.	2,400
Other small miscellaneous equipment	2,000
Observation/pill line window and supplies	8,800
Total Estimate	$90,000

Total – Non-Discretionary Increases – Secure Facilities $9,313,111

C. Justification

These funds are necessary to maintain basic levels of performance and care per statutory and constitutional mandates.

Contact: Greg Sawyer, Chief of Departmental Services, 425-7290
Greg.sawyer@doc.state.ok.us   6

Medical Services (continued)

sessions for the management of the treatment of Hepatitis C. Hepatology consultations are provided to ODOC at no professional fee. Treatment has become more complex, and more expensive, due to the addition of new treatment medications. Many other new medications are in the pipeline and are expected to come to market rapidly over the next few years. Therefore, the treatment of a single patient for Hepatitis C is estimated to cost $150,000 annually. PharmaCorr, the ODOC pharmacy vendor, reports that other states they have under contract are treating Hepatitis C in varying numbers, but all in numbers greater than ODOC has treated over the past year. Approximately 20 offender patients under treatment would be consistent with a Corrections standard of care at this time. As newer medications and classes of medications become available, the community and corrections standard of care for Hepatitis C is likely to drive toward increased numbers of ODOC patients receiving treatment. Though the cost of treatment is high, the cost of care for a patient with end stage liver disease is estimated to be approximately $300,000. Hepatitis C can progress to end stage liver disease over 20 to 30 years. The Centers for Disease Control estimate that up to 30% of all offenders are Hepatitis C infected.

Medical and Dental Supplies $40,000

This request is based upon continuing cost increases on disposable and durable medical equipment, such as syringes, needles, catheters, wound dressing, swabs, wrist splint, walkers, vital sign monitors, wheelchairs, etc. The CMS Healthcare Fact Sheet has predicted a 10.8 % rise in disposable supply costs and 9.6% increase in durable medical equipment costs.

Eyeglasses $14,000

Due to the aging offender population, costs to provide eyewear increased 25% in FY12 and it is anticipated these costs will continue to rise. From 2008 to 2012, the percentage of ODOC offenders who are greater than 50 years of age rose from 14.3% to 17.1%.

Transfers (Third Party Payer) $3,000,000

Payment to health care providers including hospitals, radiologists, physicians, renal services, ambulance services, and others was underfunded by approximately $4,000,000 in the FY13 work program due to budget cuts. In anticipation of a savings due to the passing of 2011 legislative session statutory changes in OS57 § 627 which pays non-network providers Medicaid rates, we anticipate this funding to be less.

Medical Services (continued)

Morton Comprehensive Health Services $500,000

ODOC is responsible for providing adequate health care services to
an increasing population of approximately 450 half-way house
offenders in the Tulsa area. Morton Comprehensive Health Services
is a federally qualified health clinic that provides complete medical,
mental health, dental and optometric services for these offenders.

Additions Required for FY 2014 that are not part of the FY 2013 Budget

Lindsay Municipal Hospital $2,000,000

Lindsay Municipal Hospital reduced their administrative fee from
10% to 7% through August 2012 due to DOC budget cuts. However,
the administrative fee recently increased to 8% for a three year
period. The additional increase equates to over $70,000 per year. In
addition, Medicare and Medicaid medical care inflation rates project
a 10 year average medical cost increase of 6.1%. Even though
Medicaid reimbursements are expected to continue, additional funds
are needed for the added services of the orthopedic clinic and
surgical care at Lindsay Hospital. These services were implemented
in FY 2012 and are increasing due to the successful reduction of the
backlog of orthopedic cases at OU. The FY 2012 Lindsey Municipal
Hospital average inpatient cost per day is $857.93 compared to
network hospital inpatient cost per day of $1,499 per the Kaiser
Family Foundation.

Total – Non-Discretionary Increases – Medical Services $9,500,000

C. Justification

These funds are necessary to maintain a sustained level of
performance and constitutionally compliant care.

Contact: Greg Sawyer, Chief of Departmental Services, 425-7290   9
Greg.sawyer@doc.state.ok.us

FY 2014 Budget Request Priority F

A. Item Description

> Restart of reduced or eliminated programs –
> Treatment & Rehabilitative Services

B. Cost

Programs
The items below were cut from the prior year Programs budget. To allow for reinstatement of offender programs, purchase of curriculum, and site visits to provide ongoing oversight of programmatic needs, the following is needed:

Treatment & Reentry Program Training and Program Evaluations	$100,000

Funding will be used for Reentry Training for unit managers, case managers and security staff and a contract for outside Program Evaluators to assess agency programs.

John Lilley Correctional Center Substance Abuse Program	$420,850

These funds would allow ODOC to reinstate the Substance Abuse Treatment Program at JLCC to provide four continuous groups of ten offenders per group on a four month rotation. The reinstatement of this program would provide treatment to approximately 240 offenders annually.

General Operating Expense	$100,000

To provide funds for programmatic curriculum to include Substance Abuse Treatment, Faith and Character, Thinking for a Change, Associates for Success, and Victims Impact.

Male Medium Security Substance Abuse Treatment Expansion	$250,000

Funds will be used to develop a 4-6 month substance abuse treatment programming for male offenders discharging from medium security. These funds would provide treatment for approximately 100 offenders annually.

Sex Offender Treatment	$125,000

Supplies and materials and technology needed for reinstatement of sex offender treatment programs at one minimum and one medium security facility.

Contact: Greg Sawyer, Chief of Departmental Services, 425-7290
Greg.sawyer@doc.state.ok.us

10

115

Treatment & Rehabilitative Services (continued)

Education

Operational requirements that have been adversely affected by cost increases

General Operating Expenses $90,500

Additional funding is needed to cover the increased costs of General Education Degree (GED) testing. The price quote provided for the 2013 GED tests is $78.00 each compared to our current cost of $26.50. The ODOC Education Unit administers 1,000 annually. The quoted price includes a discount for the agency, as the public rate may exceed $120.00. Total $30,000.

Additional funding is needed to cover expenses for leisure library and office supplies. Leisure library access is available in all minimum, medium and maximum state facilities which provide offenders with recreational and educational reading material. The annual purchase of newspapers, magazines, books, and other library supplies provides the offenders with a variety of reading material. Total $60,500.

Operating costs required for FY 2014 that are not part of the FY 2013 budget:

Professional Services $50,000

To provide funding for temporary staff providing data entry of Statewide GED's and administration of The Adult Basic Education (TABE) testing at Lexington Assessment and Reception Center.

Maintenance and Repair Expense $6,000

Additional funding for repair of aging scantron machines; these are located at 17 education units to scan and score TABE testing.

General Operating Expense $60,500

Additional funding to cover expenses for office supplies, school supplies, etc. for all educational facilities. Also to provide funding for offender testing material as required by State Statute.

Contact: Greg Sawyer, Chief of Departmental Services, 425-7290
Greg.sawyer@doc.state.ok.us

11

Treatment & Rehabilitative Services (continued)

Administration

Career Tech	$80,000

Restore funds due to prior year budget cuts to increase Career Tech programs at Elk City's Construction Technology program and Clara Waters Community Corrections Center Career Guidance & Development program. These funds will provide 20 additional slots each, as the programs are currently at half capacity.

Total – Non-Discretionary Increases – T&RS   **$1,282,850**

C. Justification

These funds are necessary to maintain a sustained level of performance.

Contact: Greg Sawyer, Chief of Departmental Services, 425-7290
Greg.sawyer@doc.state.ok.us

12

FY 2014 Budget Request Priority G

A. Item Description

Efficiency Improvements

B. Cost

Community Corrections
Expand program and treatment capabilities:

Parole conditions treatment for substance abuse/mental health	$350,000
Community Sex Offender Treatment	250,000
Substance Abuse & Alcohol Treatment Program at Union City CCC due to HB 3052 (JRI)	<u>34,000</u>
	$634,000

Total – Efficiency Improvements   **$634,000**

C. Justification

These funds are necessary to improve recidivism rates and provide enhanced levels of public safety.

Contact: Greg Sawyer, Chief of Departmental Services, 425-7290
          Greg.sawyer@doc.state.ok.us

13

118

Infrastructure and Equipment Improvements (continued)

Field Operations

Kitchen

Oklahoma State Penitentiary replace boiler in kitchen	$80,000
Lexington A&R Center replace boilers (3)	360,000
Dick Conner CC replace (2) boilers	206,230
Howard McLeod CC steam kettles (2)	25,000
Howard McLeod CC Hobart floor mixer	16,000
Howard McLeod CC heavy duty hot food tables (2)	11,200
Kate Barnard CCC freezer (Formerly Hillside CCC)	18,000
Kate Barnard CCC refrigerators (2)	21,500
Howard McLeod CC walk-in freezer	20,000
Mack Alford CC miscellaneous kitchen equipment	75,000
Howard McLeod CC walk-in freezer for warehouse	34,500
	$867,430

Laundry

Howard McLeod CC laundry steam boiler	63,000
Kate Barnard CCC commercial washers (2)	16,000
John Lilley CC large commercial washer	28,000
	$107,000

Heat and Air

William Key CC steam pipe repairs	27,000
John Lilley CC hot water tanks (4)	22,000
John Lilley CC Port-A-Cool fans (6)	19,200
Eddie Warrior CC air condition gymnasium/visiting room	26,250
Mabel Bassett CC replace heat exchange	31,000
Mabel Bassett CC replace air conditioning units (33) at $15,000	495,000
Mabel Bassett CC replace air conditioning units (8) at $5,000	40,000
Kate Barnard CCC replace HVAC system	50,000
Jackie Brannon CC "C" unit heat/cool	262,500
William Key CC cooling tower/chiller	200,000
Oklahoma State Reformatory air conditioner units (9)	27,000
	$1,199,950

Contact: Greg Sawyer, Chief of Departmental Services, 425-7290
Greg.sawyer@doc.state.ok.us

15

119

FY 2014 Budget Request Priority H

A. Item Description

   Infrastructure and Equipment Improvements

B. Cost

Community Corrections
Equipment Replacement

Walk-in Refrigerators/Freezers for 10 Facilities	$100,000
Kitchen appliances for all facilities	245,000

Community Corrections and Field Operations
Infrastructure

Electrical project at Elk City CWC	$150,000	
Frederick heat pump project	50,000	
HVAC project at Elk City CWC	50,000	
Window project at Elk City CWC	10,000	
		$260,000

Roof Repair

Kate Barnard CCC (Formerly Hillside CCC)	$262,500	
Mabel Bassett all housing and original buildings	2,557,800	
Enid CCC	75,000	
Oklahoma City CCC	75,000	
Eddie Warrior CC	583,800	
Jim Hamilton CC	177,300	
William Key CC	25,000	
		$3,756,400

Water and Waste Water Systems

Oklahoma State Reformatory water tower & water related upgrades	$1,300,000	
Jess Dunn CC water tower renovation and painting	126,000	
Joseph Harp CC lagoon aerator	7,500	
Joseph Harp CC irrigation cannon	15,000	
Eddie Warrior CC sewer grinder (Muffin Monster)	26,250	
Kate Barnard CCC sewer system replacement	220,000	
Jackie Brannon CC sewer grinder	25,000	
Howard McLeod CC sewer grinder	25,000	
Jim Hamilton CC sewer grinder	25,000	
Joseph Harp CC, Dick Conner CC and Oklahoma State Reformatory sewer grinders	150,000	
JLCC Sewage lagoon land application pump system	95,000	
Mack Alford CC lift-station pumps	11,000	
Mack Alford CC grinders	36,000	
Mack Alford CC irrigation pump and pipe	25,000	
Mack Alford CC aerators for lagoon	14,000	
		$2,100,570

Contact: Greg Sawyer, Chief of Departmental Services, 425-7290   14
        Greg.sawyer@doc.state.ok.us

Infrastructure and Equipment Improvements (continued)

Field Operations

Kitchen

Oklahoma State Penitentiary replace boiler in kitchen	$80,000
Lexington A&R Center replace boilers (3)	360,000
Dick Conner CC replace (2) boilers	206,230
Howard McLeod CC steam kettles (2)	25,000
Howard McLeod CC Hobart floor mixer	16,000
Howard McLeod CC heavy duty hot food tables (2)	11,200
Kate Barnard CCC freezer (Formerly Hillside CCC)	18,000
Kate Barnard CCC refrigerators (2)	21,500
Howard McLeod CC walk-in freezer	20,000
Mack Alford CC miscellaneous kitchen equipment	75,000
Howard McLeod CC walk-in freezer for warehouse	34,500
	$867,430

Laundry

Howard McLeod CC laundry steam boiler	63,000
Kate Barnard CCC commercial washers (2)	16,000
John Lilley CC large commercial washer	28,000
	$107,000

Heat and Air

William Key CC steam pipe repairs	27,000
John Lilley CC hot water tanks (4)	22,000
John Lilley CC Port-A-Cool fans (6)	19,200
Eddie Warrior CC air condition gymnasium/visiting room	26,250
Mabel Bassett CC replace heat exchange	31,000
Mabel Bassett CC replace air conditioning units (33) at $15,000	495,000
Mabel Bassett CC replace air conditioning units (8) at $5,000	40,000
Kate Barnard CCC replace HVAC system	50,000
Jackie Brannon CC "C" unit heat/cool	262,500
William Key CC cooling tower/chiller	200,000
Oklahoma State Reformatory air conditioner units (9)	27,000
	$1,199,950

Contact: Greg Sawyer, Chief of Departmental Services, 425-7290
Greg.sawyer@doc.state.ok.us

Representative of the amount of money diverted from schools, mental health, youth programs and other pressing needs, those who benefit from this system of greed not only disregard but contribute to the following disturbing facts taken from the Center for American Progress:[140]

- Women in federal and state custody reported being the mothers of 147,400 minor children.[141]

- Incarcerated women are more often the primary caregivers of their children before incarceration
- Incarcerated women are disproportionately victimized by emotional, physical, and sexual abuse
- Two-thirds of women in prison are incarcerated for nonviolent offenses, many drug-related crimes.
- African American women are three times more likely than white women to be incarcerated (now past tense)
- 85 to 90 percent of women, either incarcerated or under the control of the justice system have a history of domestic and sexual abuse. Many suffer from mental illness
- Many girls also enter the juvenile justice system with a history of emotional, physical, and sexual abuse.
- Youth are arrested for running away even when fleeing violent home situations. Girls are also more likely than boys to be sexually victimized while serving time in a facility.
- Women who are pregnant are often shackled during labor and delivery, risking the health of the mother and child.
- Mothers who have been convicted of drug related crimes are denied welfare payments when released

According to reports from the US Prison Bureau, the growth of U.S. prison populations have declined by 1.07%.[142] A negligible amount considering the 7.2 million U.S. citizens currently under the control of the criminal justice system via imprisonment, probation or parole. The figure does, however, give officials and prison owners a talking point when confronted by critics; "the U.S prison population has declined three years in a row". The decline is just enough to maintain hefty profits while simultaneously misleading the public, those taxpayers with marginal interest in the lives of those convicted of crimes different from their own. More importantly, whether or not intentional, the representation is misleading. While accurate in its overall assessment of prison populations in the United States, the statement gives the impression that the overall number of people placed under the custody and control of either state or federal penal institutions has actually decreased. In reality, the statistic refers to a decline in "growth" in federal prisons. The actual number of people imprisoned continues to increase. In other words, there is less growth in the growth.

In the face of growing discontent with an unjust system, the embarrassment of the rates of incarceration and the burgeoning state and federal budgets being expended on prisons, the smoke and mirrors come into plain view only when looking more closely at the data. For instance, the Bureau's 2012 report provides the following "Highlights":

- The U.S. prison population declined for the third consecutive year in 2012, from a high of 1,615,487 inmates in 2009 to 1,571,013 at year-end 2012.
- The U.S. imprisoned 27,770 fewer prisoners (down 1.7%) at year-end 2012 than at year-end 2011.
- The federal prison population increased by 1,453 prisoners in 2012 (up 0.7%), while the state prison population declined by 29,223 prisoners (down 2.1%)[143]

By combining both federal and state prison data, those benefiting from the continued trading of human capital can accurately present that the "U.S. prison population has declined". But these figures portend a much more ominous truth. Considering that the United States incarcerates 25% of the entire worlds' prison population while comprising only 5% of the overall world population, the total decline is miniscule. Additionally, California accounted for 51% of the reported decline but did not actually reduce their population. Under their efforts to reduce overcrowding, California merely directed incoming non-violent, non-sex and non-serious incarcerated men and women to jails rather than prisons, thus changing classification from "prisons to jails" for purposes of the relevant data. Further, as the full report discloses, the overall decline in the prison rate has only occurred in 1/3 of the states, with three states failing to report their data.[144] Two thirds of U.S. states continue to experience increases in prison populations. It is interesting that incarcerations for federal crimes have increased while those for state crimes overall have gone down. It is as if those committing crimes have prudently chosen which type of crime to commit. It is more likely that states, faced with the inability to continue housing ever increasing numbers, have chosen to curtail sentencing, decrease prosecutions, shift prisoners from one facility to another and change policies accordingly.

What becomes problematic with advancing the perception that the U.S. prison population is declining is that it fails to represent the reason for declining figures. Notwithstanding the extraordinary efforts of educators, non-profits and certain law-enforcement officials across the country to reduce crime, a more ominous reason underlies the decline in incarcerations. While the decline suggests that the responsible officials have implemented measures to curb crime and possibly unjust prosecutions, sentencing and incarceration, the truth is more consistent with the pressure of a changed economy. The Great Recession that identifies the global economic decline beginning in 2007, affected state economies in much the same way it did businesses and families. As the recession continued, states found themselves incapable of maintaining prisons at the same capacity as in past years. States cannot simply vote to increase their debt ceiling as does the federal government. With the reality of decreased tax bases and dwindling budgets, states began to bellow the financial burden of sustaining prison costs. Needing to justify reduction in prison populations judicial and legislative bodies began to adopt the notion of more humane treatment of non-violent offenders. While only cursory mention of cost has been made in reference to this new found humanity, the reduction in the U.S. prison population, therefore, is more a reflection of a shifting economy than it is a true shift in social and human ideology.

For instance, in January, 2008, prior to the pinch being strongly felt and noting that Missouri's "state's budget analysts predict a surplus" then Missouri Supreme Court Chief Judge, Laura Denvir Stith, called for more judges, prosecutors and public defenders in her State of the Judiciary Address for fear of "risking release of some prisoners for failure to give them a speedy trial".[145] In lauding the nationally recognized efforts of then Juvenile Court Presiding Judge, Jimmie Edwards, for increasing the speediness of trials and reducing the juvenile detention population, Judge Stith noted his efforts were saving the State "precious resources".[146] No mention was made of the young lives that were saved from the impact of being held in juvenile detention.

In contrast, as the surplus dwindled and the pinch began to be felt throughout the state's budget, the conversation changed. By 2010, the State of the Judiciary address delivered to the Missouri General Assembly was a much different tale. No longer able to maintain prisons with people convicted of non-serious crimes, then Missouri Chief Judge, William Ray Price, made a different plea. Feeling a much tighter belt and noting "the judiciary has come to this time of financial crisis already lean", Judge Price acknowledged that "the biggest **waste** of resources in all of state government is the over-incarceration of nonviolent offenders and our mishandling of drug and alcohol offenders. It is costing us billions of dollars and it is not making a dent in crime."[147] (Emphasis added) Judge Price went on to reference the staggering increased costs in - incarcerating individuals since shortly after coming to the bench in 1994. Almost two decades later, when the cost of over incarcerating thousands of human beings for non-violent offenses far exceeded the state's ability to pay, the need to treat them less punitively finally became a priority. The cautionary tale exemplified by these two contrasting positions should warn of future plans. These two judicial addresses, one ready to increase prosecutions (and provide more public defenders who, by inference, would not result in the same level of releases as those constitutionally mandated) and one championing more just treatment of the accused, exemplify how a change in the economy can create a change in policy. Unless this warning is heeded and substantive change in attitude towards the judicial system in the United State is diligently pursued, this country will eventually witness a resurgence in incarcerations and, as a result, a resurgence in crime. The economy will rebound, it always does. And when that occurs, there will be no limit in efforts to line the pocket of friends and contributors while devastating entire communities. If there was ever an "urgency of now" it is now while those whose intent is guided more by dollars than it is by the divine. It is now while government coffers mandate shifts toward more civil, just and humane treatment of those who society failed and later were fed to the wolves.

Considering the aforementioned shifts in incarcerations, suggesting that crime is controlled because those who commit the crimes have been conveniently locked away is a disturbing fallacy. Crime goes on behind bars even more so than outside. But label those who have succumbed to the neglect of society as criminals, inmates, prisoners or offenders, and in the minds of all but their children and others who love them, their fate no longer counts. Shuttered away in convenient concrete tombs, the crimes that take place within warrant little concern. Most go unreported. In reality, crimes take place in prisons and at higher rates than in the general population. Whether guilty or wrongfully charged, brothers, fathers, sons, daughters, nieces, nephews, aunts, uncles and even grandfathers are being victimized at alarming rates. Shifting the crime from one location to another does not eliminate the element of crime, it simply redefines the place. That is not resolution, that is geography. Statistics are skewed and present only that which those who profit want to show. Pretend crime has gone down, and it has, but only to those who vote.

Prisons are breeding grounds for crime. They are universities of criminality. Many enter on charges of possessing marijuana and graduate with a degree in selling cocaine. Others arrive convicted of breaking car windows and leave knowing how to steal the car. Women and men alike are raped daily, fights, brutal assaults, forced gladiator matches, thefts and murders all occur under the watchful eyes of under paid guards. Fueling the lack of data is not only a culture of silence, it is a lack of concern for those who are locked away.

In an article appearing in The Economist in 2012, the writer quotes, Adam Gropnik's damning feature in The New Yorker.

127

> *"Statistics are notoriously slippery, but the figures that suggest that violence has been disappearing in the United States contain a blind spot so large that to cite them uncritically, as the major papers do, is to collude in an epic con. Uncounted in the official tallies are the hundreds of thousands of crimes that take place in the country's prison system, a vast and growing residential network whose forsaken tenants increasingly bear the brunt of America's propensity for anger and violence. Crime has not fallen in the United States—it's been shifted."[148]*

In other words, as, Gropnik states in his article, "[i]f America's penal system as a whole amounts to a crime against humanity, maybe that ought to count for something, too."[149]

As one who has been victimized by just about every crime imaginable, I am not one to ignore the extensive impact that crime has on a person, families and the community or take lightly the damage that it does to one's psyche and sense of security. While acknowledging that truth, however, it is equally important to understand the larger picture. When considering the significance of a list that claims to identify The Top Ten Most Dangerous Cities, we must acknowledge that crimes committed do not just take place on the streets of Chicago or Detroit but in corporate board rooms and prison cells.

Recently an email was received from my sister-in-law, a Reservist serving overseas. In describing various aspects of a developed island in Honduras, the following was shared about crime.

> *"In the islands of Roatan, the crime is very low.*
> *The prison system works to keep you from breaking*
> *the law. The prisons provide no food or bedding.*
> *The prisoners sleep on the floor, 7 (sic) people to a*
> *cell, no food or water provided. If you don't have*
> *family or friends to bring you food, you don't eat.*
> *If you don't have family to bring you blankets, you*
> *sleep on the cold concrete floors."*

In its simplicity, this description of both the level of crime, even in the midst of poverty, and the system used to curtail it, suggest that prisons used as a deterrent to crime rather than as a vehicle for wealth, has a much greater rate of success. Though not a scientific or compassionate approach to reducing crime, the methodology seems logical. Segregation from the rest of society and the utter discomfort of no food, water, bedding or bed. Without question this approach to crime in the United States would be immediately declared as unconstitutional as being cruel and unusual punishment under the 14th Amendment. Yet, over two million people are subjected every day to a system that confines them for unusually lengthy times, and subjects them to rapes, fights, disrespect, disease, and more. In comparison, a cold hard floor seems inviting.

Chapter 6

WHY DO BLACK KIDS SHOOT?

"Sticks and stones may break my bones but words will never heart me."

~ *Old children's rhyme*

Sticks and stones may break my bones but words will never hurt me is a rhythmic retort spouted by many a child for generations. It serves as a convenient shield to deflect the pain of insults hurled by another. In reality it serves only as a momentary diversion, a means to escape an unwanted attack. Sticks and stones may break our bones but words deflate our spirit. Words hurt. Names categorize, demean and debilitate.

Experts have become very sophisticated in understanding gang signs, gang graffiti and gang clothing, yet remain completely oblivious to understanding the gang members themselves. Forgetting these young men and often, young women, are our children, gang members are labeled with names like thugs, gangbangers, wannabes or hood rats. Despite complaints of their activities, the names do not reflect an expectation that they will rise. Too often it becomes more important to catch gang members after the crimes are committed than it is to hear their cry for help before. More time is spent trying to catch them in the act of crimes than in trying to learn their names and see their hearts. Names hurt.

When teenage boys choose to create a gang then name it The Gutter Boys, it should be apparent that their self-concept of being worthless trash from the gutter requires society to take inventory of exactly how deeply they have been failed. To add insult to injury, the names they are called by everyone from preachers to reporters, contribute to a sense of worthlessness, of a sense of not fitting in.

During a radio program in which I was asked why Black kids like to shoot and why they like guns, my patience was worn thin. The questions themselves seem to suggest that the NRA was the mastermind of a gang of Black youth, that shooting was inherent in their genes. Understandably the sanitization of American history has blurred the vision of past deeds. It did not, however, erase the memory of those old enough to have experienced much of what took place. The days of segregated lunch counters, housing and buses have not long past.[150] Discrimination in employment and degradation in every aspect of life is still evident to this day.

Psychological studies abound about those things that are necessary for children to develop into well rounded adults.[151] Articles have been written about the importance of diet, of two parent families, about reading at an early age, even about eating dinner at the table. In an article appearing in the magazine *Parent,* a list of seven criteria was listed. First among the recommendations was: "The key to raising a well-rounded child is to establish a solid support system at home so that she grows up satisfied with her achievements and ambitions."[152] As usual, emphasis was placed on encouragement, respect, praise, reading, eating together and sleep. In most of the accompanying photos, primarily of whites, the environment was optimum; clean, quiet and attractive. Parental involvement was a must.[153] Yet, having some sense of the poverty, discrimination, violence, neglect and parental incarceration that millions of Black children endure, experts still scratch their heads and wonder why Black children do not thrive. Like the radio host and his listeners who just did not understand why there are drive-by shootings almost every day, those who have led privileged lives of being white, remain oblivious to the hate, disrespect, oppression, violence and exploitation that has been wrought in the African American community. They conveniently forget the lynchings, bombings, beatings, burnings, tarrings, castrations and other atrocities that not only affected the parents and grandparents of these youth but indirectly affect them, too. To further exacerbate those problems passed from generation to generation,[154] African American children are far more likely to be subjected to the effects of drug abuse, alcoholism, moral decay, high mortality, divorce, abuse, neglect, separation, anxiety, trauma, and crime that evolved from those past and present acts. All intentionally orchestrated in African American communities to destroy the social fabric, eliminate as many as possible and increase the prison population.[155] It is a slow and deliberate genocide that has taken millions of Black lives since pre-emancipation slavery.[156]

While the choice is made to spend an average of $27,528[157] annually to incarcerate the most wounded members of society rather than to send them to a state college at the average cost of $13,297,[158] there is no wonder why youth rebel with violence. Those who eventually maim and kill were always aware of the inequities in their lives. They notice that more time is spent trying to catch them doing wrong on occasion, than on seeing the pain they suffer every day. They notice that more time is spent looking at their "pants on the ground" than looking them in the eye and seeing the promise that lies beneath the hurt. While the inane question of why Black kids shoot is being asked, another generation of gangs are spawned to seek redress in guns.

It is mindless chatter to continually wonder why youth have not met expectations when expectations are low. As the most failed and neglected members of our society gang members are spoken of as if another species. There are consequences to be paid. Names have impact and people tend to rise to expectations. If the words spoken over teens are that of death and destruction, they will deliver death and destruction. If violence is to stop, so must the names. If affirmative acts to imprison young Black boys and men are to be countered, it is imperative that every outrageous crime be seen as a desperate plea for help. Playing cops and robbers will do no more than fill prison beds. A moment's interest in the life of youth can peel back years of pain and unleash talent buried beneath a neglected and abused soul. It can also save the next victim of crime and the cost of locking him up.

Some of the most brilliant minds in the world gather in hundreds of university campuses across the country studying the whys and hows of criminal behavior. Data is gathered, analyzed, shared, dissected and written about in scholarly articles year after year. Conventions are convened and seminars conducted. Yet, despite all of the scholarly review, the rates of incarcerations continue to climb. From the time private prisons began hawking incarcerations, the United States' ranking as the number one nation in the world in education has been replaced with being the number one nation in incarcerating its citizens. Education, in contrast, has dropped to 22.[159] Currently incarcerating one out of every 10 citizens, the next closest country is far from matching U.S. numbers. Even China, with more than a billion citizens, incarcerates less than half that as the United States. Clearly something is wrong.

While those who profit from the ever increasing population of incarcerated fathers, mothers, neighbors and children, others stand by and watch neighborhoods decline. They watch children seek a sense of family from gangs that provide the belonging and safety that should be the exclusive purview of homes. While those who profit from prisons line their pockets by building more prison beds, dispensing more prison garb, producing more prison food, outsourcing more prison guards, furnishing more prison maintenance, equipping more prison vehicles and providing more prison management, the children left behind suffer the social and economic consequences that result.

Despite that prisons are proven failures at deterring crime, politicians gain votes with campaign slogans of being tough on crime. They lure supporters with promises of tougher laws and accept contributions made by those with prison interests. Too many laws are enacted based on influence peddling rather than in the best interest in the state. As data has shown, the laws put more neighbors in jail and keep them there for longer times - more prisoners, longer terms, bigger profits. With growing inequities and unfairness in stops, arrests, prosecutions, convictions and sentencing, more youth and adults alike become angrier, less employable and better educated in committing crime. The response to a child who grows up in an abusive home, who lacks the discipline of a father, is influenced by one who was raised in a gang, who lives in poverty and longs for the presence of a parent who is forced to work two jobs to compensate for the other in prison, who is traumatized by neighborhood killings and neglected by us all, is to punish him for lashing out in a desperate plea for help.

With one out of every ten African American men in their twenties being under some form of criminal supervision and the incarceration of mothers more than doubled in recent years, it is not surprising that one out of every four African American youth age 14 or older has at least one parent in prison. Knowing that one fourth of African American teens grow up during their most formative years with one or both parents in prison, it is not surprising that the high school drop-out rate has doubled for African American males in the last decade and has tripled for African American females. It should not be surprising that with high school drop-outs earning 230% less than those who graduate, that African American teens make up 60% of teen prison populations; or that their anger over poverty, abuse, neglect and lack of parental direction has resulted in 60% of those being imprisoned for violent crimes. The more pertinent question is not why do Black kids shoot, the question is: Why is greed allowed to prevail?

Indeed, the parceled success of African Americans previously reserved for whites, has actually aided the growth of an industry exceeding that of chattel slavery both in numbers and in dollars. Though mandated by law, desegregation and anti-discrimination laws, while intended to provide equal access and opportunities for African Americans and other minorities, the unintended consequence has been the destruction of many social constructs inherent in the African American community. School desegregation ultimately shifted thousands of highly educated African American educators away from "ghetto schools" into those predominantly white. They took with them not only a plethora of talent and intellect but a genuine concern for their students' success. Those educators were not only preeminently qualified in the field of education but also had an understanding and commitment to the education of African American students. With that shift of those charged with the education of African American students, also came a shift in the ratio of educators who had the welfare of those students as a priority. African American students both in predominantly Black schools and in those predominantly white became faced with a new form of discrimination: that of being relegated to second class students.

Desegregated schools also provide states the opportunity to manipulate tests, targeting questions that not only subvert the African American experience but send subliminal messages of inferiority. Text books have been written and curriculums crafted that, among other things, continue to white wash the historical truth of slavery, peonage, Jim Crow and modern injustices against African Americans in the United States and overlook the many accomplishments. For all but a percentage of select students who are strongly rooted in their heritage, self-image and family support, messages of inferiority and inability are inherent in curriculums structured to give educators little, if any, latitude to provide enhanced perspectives.

For some who work with troubled youth the term gang wannabes is often bandied about. The term refers to teenagers who "aspire" to be gang members but are not considered "the real thing". Its use questions the wisdom of those who use it and gives meaning to the Biblical passage [s]ome people make cutting remarks, but the words of the wise bring healing." Prov. 12:18

Too many times those charged with keeping the community safe have actually challenged self-proclaimed gang members to step up their game. They tell them they are not "real" gang members, that they are really *just* "Wannabe's". In one fell swoop, those public servants fail to recognize the need to belong. They challenge teens to meet the criteria of "true" gang members and elevate gangs to a level to which one would want to aspire. For many youth with nothing to lose, such a challenge would be met with acceptance, the result, a "real" killing, a "real" rape, a "real" act of vandalism or robbery. And then begins a "real" game of cops and robbers.

But despite the inference above, even hard core gang members are truly Wannabes. They wanna be loved just like everyone else. They wanna be awakened in the morning to a mother's smile, a home cooked meal, and a father ready to leave for work. They wanna be in the same house longer than a few months before yet another eviction, another school and another set of acquaintances. They wanna be respected, to be hugged and kissed without sexual innuendos; to have their talents appreciated, to be called without being called out of their names. They wanna be with their fathers, or at the very least to know who their fathers are.

The children referred to as hood rats wanna be lovingly corrected by neighbors and disciplined at school. They wanna be held accountable for their actions by adults who are accountable for theirs. They wanna be told the truth and have the truth told to them. They wanna have promises kept. They wanna be able to look up to police as the ones who protect them and to judges who are fair. They wanna be in the presence of adults who act like adults. They wanna be rich and famous and have someone show them how. They wanna be a part of something bigger than themselves.

They wanna be able to learn without having their race obliterated from text books or to feel that excelling in trade school is just as respected as excelling in college. They wanna be talked to, laughed with and heard. They wanna be a part of the joke not the brunt of it. They wanna be encouraged, inspired and believed in. They wanna be looked in the eye not at their pants on the ground. They wanna be with a young lady who refuses to be called a bitch; who will not put out at the threat of being left, who will love them without the bling. They wanna be married to the girl next door not the momma of everybody's babies.

They wanna be at home without a new man lying in their mother's bed or yet another woman wanting to lay down the law. They wanna be able to grow up without their credit already ruined because mamma turned on the electric or bought a new stove using their social security number. They wanna be considered for jobs other than fast food cooks or dishwashers. They wanna be the first hired and the last fired. They wanna be in churches where the women in the front row is not flirting with the pastor and the pastor actually lives by the Word. They wanna be in families where their grandparents are grandparents not sole care givers and only source of support. They wanna be in homes where their parents' ambitions take a back seat to them; where their fathers are not burning the midnight oil or keys to a car traded for quality time. They wanna be the sons who follow in their fathers' footsteps, who respects their vows and the mother they love. They wanna be in families where their fathers are not in prison, their big brothers on probation, their uncles in a county jail or their grandfathers hocking their homes to post bail. They wanna be the big brother or sister their siblings look up to for something other than a drive-by shooting, selling drugs or carrying a roll.

They wanna be around the table on Thanksgiving Day surrounded by parents, grandparents, cousins and aunts, uncles and friends. They wanna be the one to claim the drum stick first and sit back too full to clear the table. They wanna be around a Christmas tree opening gifts their parents bought and passing out kisses of thanks. They wanna be watching the football game with their dads and uncles or gathered in the kitchen with mom. They wanna be the things they dream of, firemen, doctors, electricians, lawyers, teachers, scientists, professors and judges. They wanna be architects and bankers, business owners and artists. They wanna be biologists, lawmakers, engineers and physicists, landscapers and authors. They wanna dream and be like everyone else. They wanna have a childhood while still a child.

They wanna be old someday and see the fruit of their work. They wanna be grey haired and wise, the patriarch of their family. They wanna be able to retire with healthy portfolios - their money working for them rather than them still working for their money. And just like everyone else, they wanna be dreamers and have a chance to see their dreams come true. Why do Black kids shoot? They shoot because they just wanna be.

Chapter 7

SAVE THE CHILDREN

"For these are our children. We will all profit by, or pay for, whatever they become."

~ *James Baldwin*

A s 2012, rolled around, there were only a hand full of people who knew the name of Trayvon Martin, at least on a national level. The population of his hometown, in fact, was smaller than most high schools of those who would learn his name. But on February 26, 2012, Trayvon Martin was destined to become a household name. The reality of his tragic killing and the failure of the police to take action against the man who pursued and killed him, resurrected a languishing movement for broad civil rights. The brazen disregard for the life of an innocent 17 year old, a teenager doing no more than walking home from the store, was more than a country could bear. Indeed, news of the lack of action against a grown man who disregarded both written and verbal instructions not to follow the teenager or to carry his gun, quickly made its rounds around the world.

For months, the name Trayvon Martin was a household name. Television, newspapers, pulpits and water cooler conversations included reference to his name. Everyone weighed in. The ire of the country was raised, giving attention to issues that have long plagued the African American community; profiling, harassment, random shootings, killings and consistent failure of the legal system to bring justice to those who take the lives of anyone Black. Anchors and journalists of every race lodged questions with a persistence and intensity rarely seen. That in itself was indicative of progress. Even as recently as a decade ago, the loss of a young Black life would have been swept under the rug and nothing more said. In reality, that is exactly what happened, until word leaked out. The outrageous facts of this case had been kept a dark secret of an obscure town in Florida. The 911 recording, the police report, the admission of the killing, an unproven, self-serving statement of self-defense and the unilateral conclusion of a police chief to release the suspect and make no referral for prosecution, all filed away and considered closed.

As many concluded from the limited facts finally released, Trayvon Martin was stalked and killed by George Zimmerman. The nightmare for African American parents everywhere had just begun. For millions of parents whose Black sons walk the streets of America, unarmed, with or without hoodies, the death of Trayvon Martin was not simply the loss of his life but the crystallization that innocent African American teenagers are increasingly confined to their homes by widespread intimidation, harassment and potentially murder. For millions of Americans the tragedy in Trayvon Martin's death is that the life of a young African American man still has little value in this country; that his killer has little more to do than claim self-defense and walk away with not even a slap on the hand. The message sent loud and clear –there's a free for all on African American males.

Had the tables been turned, few African Americans doubt that Trayvon would have been immediately arrested, tried and convicted. Had Trayvon defied written instructions not to carry a weapon while acting as a neighborhood watchman; had he defied the direct verbal instructions of the police dispatcher to *not* pursue the suspect, had he referred to the suspect using the same multiple racial references and a racial slur; had he used excessive force against an unarmed white teen, they not only would have arrested him, no matter his defense, they would have begun to stack the deck against him looking for federal and state charges that would have added to the prison numbers that show African American men incarcerated at a rate six times that of whites.[160] This case exemplifies exactly how that occurs. Whites walk, charges against Blacks get stacked.

Despite the implausible statements made by Zimmerman during his nearly five minute 911 call; his decision not to drive away when Trayvon purportedly walked toward him and Zimmerman's ultimate decision to exit his car and approach someone he felt was armed and on drugs, the police Chief bought his story of self-defense. Indeed, if the tables had been turned, they would have combed that very tape for enough evidence to make a case for premeditated murder. Yet Zimmerman walked. Not much has changed from the time that the Virginia legislature protected slave owners, or indeed, any white person, from prosecution for killing a slave when resisting him. In 1705, the 1669 Virginia statute previously referenced was amended to read:

And if any slave resist his master, or owner or other person, by his or her order; correcting such

143

slave, and shall happen to be killed in such correction, it shall not be accounted felony; but the master, owner, and every such other person so giving correction, shall be free and acquit of all punishment and accusation for the same, as if such accident had never happened.[161]

In reading that statute and understanding its import, it is important to understand that neither slaves nor free Negroes were considered "persons" for purposes of enjoying certain rights. While any white person had the right to kill a slave in the process of correcting him, that same right did not inure to any Black. No matter how severely beaten, no slave had the right to defended themselves. And so it went with Trayvon Martin. Despite the language of the Stand Your Ground law, the outcome of the trial is proof positive that in the eyes of many white Americans a Black male has no right to defend himself against aggression.

The outcome of the Zimmerman trial, the inequities in arresting, prosecuting, convicting and sentencing Blacks as opposed to whites for similar crimes, mirrors the Virginia amendment in practice if not in words.[162] As statistics have historically proven, the fiat of prosecutors, judges and juries will far more often than not result in the application and interpretation of the so-called Stand Your Ground laws, acquitting a white man for killing a Black than it will for a Black in killing a person of any race. The consequence of this reality is a high degree of risk suffered by Black males by the anger and dissension created between certain whites and Blacks, the racial animosity fueled by current laws and the outcome of an unjust system.

Yet, despite the rapid increase in incarcerations as well as the escalation of violence and homicides, there are many African Americans who believe their educational degrees and their escape to the "safety" of suburban upper class neighborhoods protects their sons from the threat of incarceration or threat of being profiled. Most, it is believed, have had "the conversation", that moment when a parent sits down with their African American son when he comes of age and warns him of the very real possibility of being stopped, harassed, beaten and even arrested by police simply for "driving while Black". While white parents have "the talk" about sex, Black parents have it about race. As pointed out by a superintendent of a large, predominantly African American school district, even middle school African American students are routinely stopped and searched by police, expanding the notion even to children "walking while Black".

The over-incarceration of both Black men and women, fueled by a biased news media that long associated crime with African Americans, has created a culture that puts every Black citizen at a higher risk of crime. Neither age nor socio-economic status serves to protect African Americans from errant bullets, targeted crime or over-zealous police. In deed during what felt like a week from hell, this author experienced a series of staggering news that left a legacy of death and pain. The almost unbelievable account is as follows:

A Week from Hell

On a beautiful Saturday afternoon on March 12, 2011, hundreds of people filled the pews of Friendly Temple

Church in St. Louis, Missouri. They were there to pay tribute to a host of community leaders and to solicit volunteers to serve as mentors to area youth. Denise Thimes, an internationally known Jazz singer, was on the rostrum of those performing. Following the program, I greeted her, gave her a hug and complimented her typically outstanding performance. Two weeks later, Thimes was back on the same stage sharing her enormous talent to a church filled to capacity. Unlike the previous appearance filled with hope for the future, this time she was singing at her sister's funeral, the victim of a stray bullet that followed a rash of homicides in those interim two weeks. At 39, Patrice Thimes was dead, leaving two children, including a five year old son. Fitting the reality created in many inner neighborhoods, three African American teenagers have been charged in her death.

The Friday before this unexpected tragedy, my high school classmates and I attended a birthday party for one of our classmates. It was the first since high school we had done so and one of the very few times we would meet over the course of any given year. Making the event rarer was the presence of a classmate who never made any of the previous gatherings. This was the first. Quiet and unassuming in high school, she had led a similar life since.

As we all made our rounds, I hugged her and shared how glad we were she had come. For one special night we reminisced, laughed, and said our goodbyes. The following Saturday, on March, 19, 2011, exactly two days after the tragic murder of Patrice Thimes, word came that our classmate's 22 year old son had been killed. Shot multiple times while sitting in his car, he left a new born daughter just

146

a few days old. Three months into the new year, Craig Underwood was identified as homicide #23.

While reeling from the untimely death of Patrice, my classmates and I made plans to visit Craig's mother the next day. Before leaving church, however, I waited as usual to hug and greet my brother-in-law, the organist and choir director at church. Waiting longer than I normally would, I finally gave him a hug and wished him a good week. Grieving from not one but now two untimely deaths I called my classmates and headed home to meet. We arrived at our friend's home finding her in shock and yet, reassuring us with her familiar smile. Nearby was her daughter and the many young friends who had gathered at her home. They paced the front yard, heads still shaking in utter disbelief. Mothers are not supposed to bury their children but far too often African American mothers do.

Still needing to vent and remain together, we decided to return to my home. As the reality of the week's events sank in, we sat recounting the gentleness of our classmate, a young woman rarely seen without a smile. We wondered how such a tragedy could take her only son, her of all people. We talked about just seeing her, about Denise Thimes just singing the week before, how Patrice had just taken her niece and nephew to dinner and had just dropped them off at home. We talked about the violence that suddenly hit close to home. As we prayed, talked and grasped for answers my phone rang. Within seconds it felt like I had been transplanted to another world. I could barely make sense of anything. My legs weakened. My stomach got sick. As my classmates watched the blood drain from my face and perplexity turn to horror, I shared the tragic news. My

147

brother-in-law's mother had just been killed. The brother-in-law I hugged just hours before, quite possibly just as the murder took place. Just as his mother was returning home from church, a 20 year old man she was known to help, shot her in the head and took her car. At 88, this quiet, unassuming woman was dead. The third of three violent gun deaths in the course of four days. All had hit home.

There are other murders I could include among these. That of my board members 18 year old son the following year, or that of another board member's father years before, both which have deeply affected their families. The list could go on. But these three murders brought with them proximity in time, the similarity in violence and the ages of all three. Two were much too young to die and one, who at 88 deserved much more dignity than to die lying in her own blood.

And then there were the hugs. As if to emphasize how easily death can touch our lives, I had just hugged Patrice Thimes' sister, Craig Underwood's mother and Gladys Cockrell's son. None of us suspecting at the time what heart ache awaited just days, even hours away. I choose to include these three murders because just like Trayvon Martin, they were senseless, attributed to guns and targeted those we would least expect. Despite an increase of federal incarcerations of more than 500% in 30 years,[163] the increase in crime and violence is palpable. These successive murders illustrate how vulnerable we all are and how angry, desperate and violent incarcerations have made this country.

Like Trayvon Martin, Craig Underwood came from a family of deep faith. His parents are still together, they had always lived a middle class life. His mother attended a private, predominantly white, all girls, Catholic, high school. They attended church, they attended school. They worked. Like any middle class family they supported each other and they dearly loved their only son.

Patrice Thimes came from a close knit family. Her father was a local legendary disc jockey who entertained audiences for decades, her brother his father's legatee. Her sister, Denise Thimes, has sung for presidents, dignitaries and the Queen. Her parents remained together until their mother's death. A family of strong faith, they worked together and prayed together.

For almost nine decades Mrs. Cockrell was a woman of faith. Married until her husband's death, her well-kept home reflected the values she passed on to her son; he an educator, accomplished musician, and church music director, his wife a principal of a school not far from his mother's home. His daughter was just weeks into her second semester as a pre-med student at St. Louis University. Their comfortable home nestled among trees and landscaped lawns.

The desperation and effects of centuries of degradation, discrimination and over incarceration of African Americans has created such a level of violence that no amount of education, manicured lawns or well-appointed homes will protect anyone from the fallout. In 1955, it was Emmitt Till, savagely beaten with racist intent. In 1963, hate killed four little girls bombed in a Birmingham church. In 1998, it was James Byrd Jr., drug to his death by three supremacists, in 1999, there was Rodney King, savagely beaten by police and Amadou Diallo killed by 17 of 41 bullets fired by New York

City's "finest". There were thousands more before them and thousands more since, the victims of hate and misguided fear.

The crime that permeates every aspect of life in America is robbing its citizens of as much freedom as it does property. Despite the staggering increase in incarcerations, the freedom and safety taken for granted before the onslaught began have been stolen with more consistency than stereos and guns. No longer do couples walk in the moonlight, swing on front porches or sit in parked cars. Homes have become fortresses with alarms, bars, locked doors and windows shut tight. Police wear bullet proof vests and everyone else stays inside. Few children walk to school and even fewer play outside. Stray bullets and predators choose victims of every age. But for the immeasurable freedoms surrendered every day, crime would be even worse. Incarcerations have not made us safer, they have only made a select few very rich.

So entrenched in fighting the everyday struggles wrought in the lives of so many African Americans that it is difficult to see the freedoms denied. Many have forgotten what it is like to pursue dreams. Some have never known to try. Many have forgotten what it was like to leave doors unlocked or to feel fresh air through open windows. Generations have never known. Black children inherently know not to run on city streets for fear of being held suspect for some unknown crime. With Black children nine times more likely to have a parent incarcerated, the increase in teen pregnancies and sexually transmitted diseases should be of no surprise. Children left to fend for themselves while single parents work two jobs, seek refuge in gangs that proliferate more crimes. Grandparents abandon their nurturing role and become the sole caregiver and provider. Generational incarceration has ravaged entire families with fathers, grandfathers, uncles and brothers in prison for decades. When prison profits dropped, women became the target. The incarceration of women has grown by 800% in the last 30 years, recently far outpacing the increased rate of the incarceration of men.[164]

Feeling powerless over a system that has imbedded itself in politics and virtually every way of life, America accepted as the norm the over incarceration of Blacks. After valiant battles during the civil rights era, complacency set in. Many whites hung their hats on civil rights given and Blacks rested theirs on the civil rights gained. In the interim, those who lost battles both in the Civil War and in the courts, took out paper and pen and wrote a new legacy of hate. The result of such complacency is a criminal justice system replete with stilted laws, over-zealous police, unethical prosecutors and over worked public defenders. While laws target African Americans and Hispanics, white America commits crime far in excess of minorities and hides them in the cloak of corporate law.

Too many African American children have been handed a world without hope. Amidst ram shackled homes, they see a world where their neighbors' college degrees secure no more than underpaid jobs, where their brothers die young and their fathers sit in jail. They are surrounded with neighborhoods of vacant houses, boarded windows and shuttered doors. They are told that jobs are scarce and college is out of reach.

While multi-million dollar homes rise up by the thousands in suburban neighborhoods, late model cars pack downtown lots, highways are paved and high rise buildings and prisons go up, Black children are told the "economic crisis" must close their schools. They are handed Air Jordans and told to go away. The only economic crisis we have in this country is that of greed and moral decay. Judges sell their souls to the devil and the lives of our youth down the river. Corporations and speculators invest in privatized prisons and write laws to increase their stock. Every day, in hopelessness, African American families turn over their sons, and increasingly their daughters, to the prison profiteers and shed quiet tears that change nothing. Legislators pump sugar into our children then mandate pills to calm them down. Millions are poured into the pockets of those who demanded segregation so African American children can wait at bus stops to go to integrated school. While Africa American children struggle to survive, others get rich from the buses they own, the gas that fills them and repairs that are made. In the meantime African American children pass affluent suburbs and return home to so much less. Money is taken from Black neighborhood schools and Blacks get to drive the bus. Minimum wage, maximum loss.

When Sesame Street shifts from teaching the ABCs to teaching about incarcerated parents, we see the depths to with this country has fallen.[165] Despite the massive nature of a system born to replace an economy lost to emancipation, it is imperative to act. Despite the gains made by some, there are far too many left behind. The longer it takes to act, the more entrenched the system becomes, the more our children will suffer.

Chapter 8

TOWARDS A LESS PUNITIVE SOCIETY

"Train up a child in the ways that he should go and when he is old he will not depart from it."

~ *Proverbs 22:6*

In a small park in St. Louis County, Missouri, there is a metal sign affixed to the top of a pole. It reads, "Do Not Litter. Littering is Punishable by a fine of $500 or a year in jail." A year in jail for discarding an empty can, allowing a potato chip bag to alight with the swiftness of a summer wind; for pitching an empty wine bottle amidst the thickets or grass. Whether imprisonment or even a fine has been used as a method of litter control is unknown to the author. But the mere suggestion that jail could be the consequence for tossing trash, that the threat of jail is our society's knee jerk reaction to virtually every behavior that might moderately offend the sensibilities of others, is telling of our attitude toward crime, prison and behavior modification. It is primitive at best.

In ancient times, in less "civilized" countries, various means of punishment were used to deter the unwarranted behavior of others. Stonings, beheadings and public floggings were frequently used to punish perceived violations of moral and civil codes. In these modern times we find such deterrents as crude methods designed by unevolved men. Yet, in the United States of America numerous laws are enacted, designed by argulus men and a handful of women that reflect an evolution of thinking not much more advanced. As exemplified by the park sign, engaging in such intentional or mindless acts as littering a park or street, a person could ultimately lose their low paying job. (Well paid executives do not often empty their cigarette trays outside their car doors or pitch McDonald's wrappers out of their windows. Well paid executives seldom go to jail.) It is normally those with low paying jobs, the last to be hired and the first to be fired, who use Mother Earth as their personal trash receptacle. And, based on the sign prominently displayed, their ill-thought decision could mean a year in jail -a year away from their children, spouse or ailing parent. It could mean foreclosure, a repossessed car or loss of income for those he or she will no longer pay. It would certainly mean thousands and thousands of tax payer dollars paid to teach a single litter bug not to throw out trash. This is not to defend those who would fill our parks with empty bottles and useless trash. The past has taught us those consequences. In days gone by, the curbs of city streets were caked with piles of trash. Sidewalks were buffeted with paper, cans and discarded cigarettes. Bags blew across well-manicured lawns and broken bottles were strewn at the base of playground swings. There is nothing about littering that anyone would defend as good citizenry. But using the threat of jail for something as vapid as littering does no more than reflect a desperate society lacking control of the errant child it raised. It diminishes the value of a system that places more emphasis on punishment than it does on solving problems and reflects an inability to devise meaningful ways to build stronger communities rather than tear them down.

Such signs epitomize the extent to which incarcerations are used as a means of control. Lacking sufficient public outcry, civic leaders go unchallenged to find less punitive means to achieve compliance. It can be assumed that manufacturing and posting signs that threaten confinement is an easier route than seeking more positive solutions. Providing more trash cans that local artists and students paint would not only provide easier access for depositing trash but would beautify the streets and parks and create a sense of ownership. Creating public service announcements that appeal to the greater good of all are just a few alternatives that could achieve the same goal.

Despite our advancement in science and technology, this society is so quick to punish for even the most minor offenses that often it fails to explore possibilities. Centuries after escaping the oppressive rule of other countries, the United States has not evolved beyond primitive rule. "Do as I say, or else." While children are taught that practice makes perfect and repetition is encouraged as a means of correcting mistakes in sports, music or the arts, jail is often the response when a Black child errs in his way. Of course, there are over zealous parents who introduce punishment in those arenas as well, castigating their less than perfect child for failing to perform with perfection, but for the most part, mature adults patiently and intelligently guide a child to practice, practice, practice. A mistake is turned to precision not by inflicting penance, but by praising that which is good and correcting that which is not. While adults are encouraged to "find the good and praise it" as a means of redirecting the misguided behavior of middle class children, those of less fortunate means are not only impugned but detained.

Finding the good

With a prison system that has wreaked a massive human toll, it is critically important to seek a healthy balance to achieving a society that respects not only the rights but the freedoms of others. Beginning in the 1950s, modern psychologists examined the abuse exacted in classrooms, detention centers, mental facilities and group homes and took the removal of punishment beyond a reasonable measure.[166] Educators and psychologists alike agree that "finding the good and praising it" is a far more effective means of achieving changed behavior than inflicting pain, though pain is often necessary when inept parenting creates a more resistant child. Recently several concerned parents made headlines when their methods of constraining their teen's behavior crossed the proverbial line; a father shot up his daughter's laptop and posted it on YouTube after discovering her YouTube tirade about his parenting. Two other parents chose to create T-shirts that gave public notice of their teenager's inclinations to steal or use drugs. Lacking more effective tools, each parent thought humiliation would result in needed change. Misguided in the eyes of many, the decisions of these concerned parents do no more than reflect the pervasive attitude toward error, castigate.

Based on the public responses to the aforementioned incidents the jury seemed to be split on the appropriateness of public humiliation to bring about positive change in a child's behavior. But as extreme as the actions of these parents may have been in the eyes of some, they at least exhibited concern and made an effort to discipline their child. Many do not. The converse of these parents who engaged in non-conventional methods of control are those who do nothing. Those who allow their children to rule the roost and force them to continue to act out until some boundary is set. Unfortunately for many, those boundaries do not come until prison bars are used. Both extremes of responding to a child finding his or her way in this vastly confusing world of morals, rules and conduct, reflect the failure of society to equip parents with adequate means of redirecting their child's actions –particularly as they enter those dastardly teen years. Children desperately need direction and boundaries and are hardwired to test parents and adults to determine their level of safety.[167] Given boundaries from the outset, providing guidelines and direction that *respects* the child's ability to make limited decisions yet restricts them from venturing into shark infested waters gives them a healthy balance of independence and safety. When children are endowed with respect for their rights, they become free to display respect for the rights of others.

Providing this balance in early years; equipping parents with the tools necessary to take and maintain control without responding in the extreme, makes it unnecessary for society to step in at later points in life to provide the control that is lacking at home. But we do not. As a society that has effectively destroyed the family structure for millions through over incarceration, we have failed to provide the guidance, nurturing and parenting skills normally passed from generation to generation. Every year billions of dollars are spent on education) with few of those dollars being funneled into the hands of African American businesses). New testing measures are devised, and countless years are spent gathering, organizing and studying data about every possible problem. Gifted students navigate through universities compiling degree after degree but still ponder where things went wrong. Pregnant teen girls were re-integrated into mainstream schools and eventually tax dollars were used to provide them with on-site day care. And yet seldom is there a class that teaches them parenting. Even the notion of teaching abstinence and restraint raises eyebrows and banners.

Admittedly, parenting is a highly personal act. It can be complicated when trying to streamline the effort into a single technique. Religion can play a large role in the manner in which a child is raised, some conflicting with others. Values and morals differ; even mannerisms are based on cultural differences. Yet there are basic, common threads that run through all methods of healthy child rearing that can be taught. There are means to raise a well-balanced, disciplined and respectful child who must and will integrate into a much larger society. The common thread that seems to weave between various cultures and produces a child who is both respected and respectful is a degree of discipline. Children who are lovingly given guidance, correction and reasonable restrictions grow up not only understanding boundaries but feel protected by them. They feel safe knowing the rules, even when those rules are restrictive or make little sense to their still developing brains. Those rules and restrictions, particularly when enforced through the sacrifice of the parent or guardian, demonstrate essential elements of both love and concern for the child. On the other hand, what seems to have failed miserably at every stage of life is a technique we have come to know as punishment. Often confused with discipline (*v* **2:** to train to control the mind and body),[168] punishment as defined by Merriam Webster is **a:** suffering, pain, or loss that serves as retribution **b:** a penalty inflicted on an offender through judicial procedure **c:** severe, rough, or disastrous treatment.[169] Absent in each of these definitions of punishment is any display of concern for its subject, any positive benefit to society or any beneficial outcome for those involved. Punishment, as it is understood and defined in this country, is nothing more than a punitive reaction to unwanted behavior. It has no basis in rehabilitation and often results more from intolerance than it does from truth. In practice it is unjustly meted out and targets those who deviate not such much in their actions as they do in their looks. Studies show that African Americans and other minorities are far more likely to be "punished" in schools, as in other arenas, than those of the dominant culture; targeted for retribution more often than others.[170] Punishment is not used for the good of society, it is used out of ignorance of more effective means.

A Punishable Offense

Indeed, if we consider the definitions of punishment above, one which implies by use of the term offender, that there has been an offense, we must dissect the word "offense". One definition of offense is "the breaking of a law or rule".[171] Such laws and rules, however, are spuriously determined and even more spuriously enforced.

As an example, I had the pleasure of accompanying two of my grandchildren to their grandparents' day lunch at school. We were seated at the lunchroom table that had been covered in plastic tablecloths for the occasion. Plastic forks and spoons had also been provided for the special meal. As we sat for an unusually long time awaiting the principal's complicated method of calling tables to the buffet, my granddaughter began quietly moving her plastic spoon and fork into various designs at her place. (This egregious act is sometimes referred to as fidgeting.) There are several operative words in the preceding sentences that give significance to what happened next. The table was *covered in plastic*, the fork and spoon were *plastic* as well, we waited a *very long time*, and she moved them *quietly* at *her place*. Despite this benign means of staving off the boredom experienced by a five year old and despite being in the presence of not just two other adults but her own grandparents, the principal came by the table and instructed her to stop playing with the fork and spoon. Need I remind the reader that we were waiting a very long time and that she was playing with the plastic fork and spoon on the plastic table cloth, quietly at her own place?

This incident is pointed out for several reasons. As a graduate of a Catholic grade school, high school and law school, (though punishment for infractions diminished greatly with the latter two) I was keenly sensitive to the arbitrary rules established by Catholic nuns and even more sensitive to the levels of punishment exacted for infractions. Apparently when we lack the ability to creatively direct a child's behavior, or lack the sense to recognize that they actually have the ability to appropriately direct their own without constant interference, there is a tendency to create rules and boundaries that have neither rhyme nor reason. Clearly this principal had failed to properly execute her carefully constructed plan and in her frustration, the only means of creating order over that which she could control was to direct my grandchild to stop quietly moving her plastic fork and spoon. Other than the very slight movement of my granddaughter's hands and wrists she disturbed no one. She was not talking. She had not alighted from her seat. There was no threat of the utensils becoming projectiles and embedding themselves in the eye of a nearby child. My granddaughter's actions were harmless, creative and quiet.

Admittedly, I initially found myself ignoring my granddaughter when she resumed her play. The admonishment was utterly senseless and caused more dissension than good. But moments later I came to my senses and was forced to join in this charade of arbitrary control. Like it or not, right or wrong, my granddaughter had been instructed to stop by an adult in authority and to remain silent set the stage for defiance of more meaningful rules in the future. As though still in school myself, I begrudgingly intervened. Fumes quietly formed between my ears as I gently placed my hand over my granddaughter's and reminded her in a quiet voice that she had been told to stop. I stopped my granddaughter not because the principal was right and not to keep her from getting in trouble had she been seen on another round past our table. I intervened to teach my granddaughter to respect authority when doing so, though unreasonable, is not a threat to her physical or mental safety. This, unfortunately, was such a case.

This story of a plastic fork and spoon is included to illustrate the significance of the word "offense". It is important to recognize this significance because a punishable offense is often no more than an arbitrary rule established by someone who has lost a sense of control, often over their own personal lives. The so called "rule" that was broken many times is nothing more than someone else's regulation designed to restrict behavior for no other reason than the chosen act being one to which they disagree. It is more about the person wielding control than it is about the offender or, in this case, even the offense. Merely, however, because of a designation of authority by someone who themselves were given a designation of authority and so on and so on, a person then becomes the object of an arbitrary punishment.

Scenarios such as these play out thousands of times a day in cities and towns across the world. Frustrated people who have little or no control over that which they feel they should, design rules and laws that restrict the behavior of others and then punish what they perceive to be violations. It also serves to fill the treasuries of those who lack other means. In the City of St. Louis, dozens of citizens routinely fill municipal courtrooms to address housing violations. Fines are assessed for failing to cut grass, having over grown shrubs or failing to remove derelict cars. Each is a matter that affects the appearance and at times, the safety of the neighborhood. Court appearances are necessary to prove compliance or to make payment on fines the owners can ill afford. A day off from work only makes matters worse. Yet, just blocks away from the scenes of these "crimes" vacant buildings line neighborhood streets by the hundreds. Broken windows, fallen bricks and the same over grown grass and shrubs that warranted citations for others sit unaddressed. Roofs cave in, foundations collapse and displaced bricks lay orphaned in neglected piles. But, for decades nothing is done. The buildings remain intact, evidence of the affect drugs and incarcerations have had in the community and reminders to those who live nearby of their hopelessness and diminished stature. More than just eyes soars that decrease the value of the few nearby homes, these abandoned properties become havens for drug deals, sites for rapes and graves for murdered bodies. Thus is the duplicity of laws. Enforcement for those who can least afford it, amnesia for those who rape the community then flee for higher grounds.

Illegal Search, No Seizure

Another such illustration of arbitrariness and abuse was shared by a thirty something African American man. Driving near a friend's neighborhood he decided to drop in for an unannounced visit. Getting no answer at his friend's door, the man turned to leave. He was immediately confronted by two policemen -both pointing their guns. Like Trayvon Martin, this man had been ambushed for no reason at all and then questioned why he was there. Discounting the veracity of the man's explanation, the officers proceeded to illegally search his car for drugs and illegal weapons. Finding none, one officer then placed his hand over the man's heart, finding it, of course, pounding. As if the man's state of heightened fear was a joke, the officer then chuckled and asked if he was scared. Although the man had no warrants nor had broken a single law, he was told to leave and to never be seen around there again. Racially profiled, illegally searched and then denied his constitutionally protected right to move freely in his own country.

As another example of over criminalization, in the State of Maryland, the mere act of parking in restricted zones of a state university not only carries substantial monetary fines, but the failure to pay becomes a criminal offense.

These types of incidences illustrate the inability of those in authority to harness their power and seek conciliatory means in which to resolve problems they perceive to exist. In the case of this young man, of Trayvon Martin, of Amadou Diallo and countless others, no laws had been broken, simply African American men walking the streets as African American men. More importantly, the latter two incidents illustrate how problems are created simply because society has grown accustomed to using punishment as a means of controlling others –even when those "others" need no control.

Punishment is so prevalent in the United States today that prisons are a greater focus than are schools. While cities with dense populations of African Americans like Philadelphia, St. Louis and Chicago have closed dozens of schools for lack of funding that both state and federal legislative bodies manage to find billions to funnel into prisons.[172] While mental institutions are closed around the country, prison beds are found to house the displaced patients,[173] but only after they have victimized unsuspecting citizens. The incentives are the same. Limit access to education and services, increase incidences of incarcerations, generate more profits. Given the thousands of ill-equipped mental patients who are sent to the streets, men and women incapable of sustaining jobs and lacking the social skills necessary to successfully survive, the chances of crimes being committed substantially increase.[174] Transfer thousands of African American students into predominantly white school districts and governing bodies gain control over their education, their self-esteem, their discipline and their allotted fees. When hostility rises in climates unprepared for the influx of students, the disparity in discipline leans toward the suspension or even expulsion of the African American student.[175] In their study of African American males in US schools, Dr. Ivory Toldson and Dr. Chance W. Lewis point out the phenomenon of African American students being disciplined far more often and more harshly than white students when engaging in the same conduct.[176]

Safe Schools

The Safe School Act added even more layers of harsh responses to children whose behavior is often no more severe than in past generations. Such is reflected in President Obama's Executive Order to counter the outcomes by, among other things, addressing school discipline that disproportionately affects African American students.[177] Under the guise of protecting the safety of students, the Safe School Act has been used to suspend hundreds of kindergarten and other students for such benign acts as hugging another first grader,[178] fashioning a gun with fingers,[179] or even hugging a best friend.[180] A five year old girl handcuffed behind her back and taken away by police is just one of many incidents of that kind.[181] A shameful display of ineptness on the part of those teachers and even more so on the part of city officials, from the school administrators to the police chief, complicit in allowing their schools to become police states.

Potentially the well-intended effort of some well-intended legislators, the Safe School Act is emblematic of a mindset of punishment. If not an intended effort to create a pool of prison candidates, The Act has certainly been used to do so. School officials and legislators alike find it easier to spend billions of dollars a year to build and maintain prisons than to spend a fraction of the cost teaching parenting skills to those victimized by a negligent and complicit society. And so goes the plan. The Safe School Act has become yet another tool to mainstream minority and other marginalized youth from schools directly to the more profitable prisons. With 60% of incarcerated youth having dropped out or having been expelled from school,[182] it is as if more value is placed on some students than it is on those expelled. Since expelled students are the ones society already failed, we add insult to injury by casting them further aside and then wait in hiding for their first mistake. Left unsupervised, unwanted, uneducated and unemployed, the students most in need of society's embrace are summarily tossed aside. In many instances they will quickly turn their anger, frustration and desperation from misconduct in the classroom to violence on the street. Everyone becomes fair game. Despite enactment of zero tolerance laws or possibly because of them, society has become less, not more safe. The staggering increases in prison populations is a crime in itself. Though many are

166

imprisoned for so-called victimless crimes, just as many leave victims in their wake. If the system is justifiably incarcerating those who commit crimes in order to protect the citizenry, statistics suggests we have miserably failed. Considering the now 2.2 million U.S. citizen currently constrained by a federal or state system, many represent actual crimes committed. With only a percentage of individuals confined to a jail or prison returning there for parole violations such as possessing a gun, using drugs or failing to pay mandated fees[183] and thousands of others wrongfully convicted as estimated by The Innocence Project,[184] the majority of those incarcerated have victimized at least one person by their crime. Hardly a number that reflects an increase in safety.

Tyler Dasher

As happens too often these days, an Amber Alert was issued for a missing child. Those who could, glued their eyes to their TV as details unfolded and updates were given. A 13 month old baby had been abducted from his home, the unidentified body of an infant had been found in nearby woods.[185] Early reports indicated the mother was young, single, and most notably, she was distraught. No one interviewed disagreed that she adored her son, that he was well cared for and that she was a good mother. News reporters were visibly shaken with the thought of a murdered baby, viewers ached over the anguish of a doting young mom. His name was Tyler Dasher, and those who watched were horrified by the crime.

As the entire area waited hours for a positive identification, the media shared comments from a host of neighbors and friends who could not express enough grief for the young mother or laud her enough for her devotion and independence. Their constant vigil throughout the day spoke to the mother's likeability and their admiration for her as a devoted parent. All perplexed as to who would take a young baby from its home and unceremoniously dump its body nearby. The cause of death had not yet been revealed.

Teams of skilled personnel scoured the neighborhood. Later their sudden absence signaled a conclusion had been drawn. Within hours of the initial report, the forensic and police investigations were announced; the young 13 month baby boy, first reported missing and then found dead, had been beaten to death by his mother, his body left in the open field within blocks of his home. The report showed no signs of past abuse. He was well nourished and by all accounts "a very happy boy".

Before the St. Louis County Police resolved the crime in record time, Police Chief Tim Fitch told reporters, "[i]t says to me it's a pretty sick person. Anybody that would take a child and leave a child in a wooded area in that condition needs to be dealt with severely by the criminal justice system." And there lies the problem. Our society has often dealt with "sick people" within the criminal justice system, not with clinical treatment. The results have been tragic for all. A sick person needs psychological evaluation, treatment and segregation from society. A sick person needs our support and understanding, not harsh treatment.

The out pouring of sympathy from reporters, friends and neighbors just the day before had suddenly changed. No longer was the distraught, young mother sympathized over the loss of her child, she suddenly became vilified. Young neighbors who, just hours before, lauded the mother's maternal attributes suddenly spewed words of anger and denunciation. News reporters no longer allowed their emotions to show, the death of Tyler Dasher was now just another story... "Tyler Dasher was beaten by his mother and his body dumped in a park." Gone was every shred of concern for the mother who admitted her role, a young woman who had given birth at 19 and who had snapped when her infant son refused to stop crying and return to sleep. There was no sympathy for the fact that the child she had cared for with such devotion had not only suffered at her own hands but was gone forever. No mention that her life was irreparably changed and that prison would bring her a life of isolation and threats. Not a single psychiatric expert was interviewed. No psychological association or criminal justice expert was given the platform to explain the ordeal. One simple message was sent – beat your child to death, you go to jail. For all the young parents within ear shot of reports or anyone else who may have a child in their care, no warning signs to look for would be given; nothing to alert them about pushing themselves too far, that too much independence is not necessarily a virtue. No list of agencies where overly stressed parents or caregivers could go for help were flashed on the screen. No reference made to website that might give helpful hints.

For the person watching who one day may have a split second snap in judgment the only restraint provided was the fact that astute investigators will discover the truth and jail will ultimately ensue. An inadequate deterrent at best. Hundreds of children are abused every year and many die from their injuries. No doubt each abuser was aware that prison would be the end result. Clearly that message had been sent to Shelby Dasher, Tyler's mother, in so many different ways, yet the death of her child was not a sufficient deterrent, neither was the thought of prison. When a person snaps all logic and judgment is gone. Like other parents pushed too far, Shelby Dasher needed compassion and help not rejection and jail.

Until we learn to be a less punitive society and begin to provide intervention rather than punishment, we will have more babies found in parks, stuffed in washing machines or roaming the streets. Until we learn to reach out to our neighbors and become the village it takes to raise a child, to live in a community of unique cultures and needs, we are destined to see more babies killed, more victims discovered and more prisons being built.

Chapter 9

WHAT'S IN IT FOR ME?

"The only thing necessary for the triumph of evil is for good men to do nothing."

~ *Edmund Burke*

Too often in this world, many stand on the side lines and ask, "What's in it for me?". They are unwilling to extend a hand unless there is something offered in return. There is a growing problem in the United States and no community is immune. At some point it will reach the doorstep of us all. The difficulty today is the sheer number of African Americans who live in a mirage of success. Their degrees and positions convince them of exclusion from crime or from prison itself. They drink the sand and believe it is water while clinging to the hope that it is. As one who witnessed six very successful, educated African American men imprisoned in rapid succession, there is no question that college degrees do not exempt even the best. Each of their white collar crimes were those for which white men are routinely given a pass. As one who witnessed a family of professionals emotionally and financially destroyed over an under-aged teenage girl dated by their son, it is obvious that virtually anyone is prey. As one who lost a law license to a system brazenly wrong, it is painfully clear that no one is exempt. If for no other reason than self-preservation, it is time to get involved.

Casting Stones

It may be easy to take the position that a "criminal" should "do the time for doing the crime" but there are few people who have not broken the law. You could rightfully cast the first stone if you have never lied on your tax returns (a federal offense), omitted property or income from a bankruptcy case (a federal offense), if you who have never given alcohol to a minor or let a minor drive, if you never lured a 16 year old to bed when you were over 17 (a state offense of statutory rape), if you who never pilfered from your job (theft) or never shoplifted, smoked weed or snorted cocaine. You might be justified in casting the first stone if you never spanked a child (modern day abuse), drank liquor under age, dropped trash in a park or never paid a prostitute for sex. You may be entitled to judge if you never transported "a child across state lines" for a rendezvous in the park, if you never stole electricity or kited a check, if you never lied on a federal or state application, failed to report income to the IRS or failed to pay a traffic ticket and never went to court. Cast the first stone if you never slipped out with groceries in your cart or switched tags on a suit, if you never sold an ounce of marijuana or kept a stash for yourself, if you never worked while receiving unemployment benefits or never claimed someone else's child as a dependent on a tax return, or bought clothing that was hot (possession of stolen goods), if you never availed yourself of a no-doc mortgage and inflated your income or changed someone's else' on an application received. Turn away if you never used prescription drugs to get high or bought an illegal gun, if you never inflated expense accounts at work, or committed adultery (still illegal in 22

172

states). Most people have committed a crime of some type and were simply never caught; even those who were, were given a second chance. There are bankers who steal billions from the customers by manipulating accounts and charging exorbitant fees and predatory lenders who bilk millions from the poorest of the poor. And most ironically, there are private prison owners who inflate their books and receive federal payments but never serve a day. Too many people find it expedient to do nothing while casting stones at those who violated the most innocuous laws. It is easy to point fingers and condemn those behind locked doors, but those pointing the fingers are likely guilty, too.

Do it for joy

In my first book, 21 Days to Joy, there is a chapter on serving others. In bold letters there is a quote from the book. "Service nourishes the soul like food nourishes the body. It is necessary for growth and essential for joy."[186] There is a great deal of truth to those words. It is impossible to grow without serving others. The more you serve, the more you grow. It is equally impossible to have joy without service to others. Happiness and joy are not the same. Happy is in the moment, joy is in the soul. Though it is best to serve simply from a genuine desire to give, if you really want to know what is in it for you, at the very least the answer is growth and joy.

The Price of Complacency

Key to dismantling this system of gross injustice and targeted inhumanity is not merely to identify those eagerly profiting from the human suffering of others, it is also to recognize the role of the good guy who does nothing. In order for any system of injustice to succeed in the face of mankind, it is necessary to have a significant majority of everyday of people stand by the wayside and do nothing. It is that complacency that has allowed the rates of incarceration to increase from 500,000 to 2.2 million in the last 30 years. When the only clamoring a legislator hears is the resounding demands of those tainted by greed, it is unlikely that those cloaked with the authority to act will do so to the benefit of the masses who remain silent. Gone are the days, if indeed they ever existed, that morality, fairness, justice, and compassion were the guiding principles of lawmakers. Gone is the notion that leadership means leading, that those given charge of the lives of millions, would fiercely defend that responsibility.

Group dynamics unfortunately have shown that even in the direst of circumstances, there is a dismal lack of individual capacity to act when the majority acquiesce. Social media and the Internet have brought together millions of people to share, discuss and weigh in on crucial issues of the day. Despite this new connectedness, however, absent a personal mandate to get involved, interest in the lives of others wanes. Experiential denial allows those who have done no wrong to pretend that such is true. It allows legislators, corporate leaders and vendors to witness the gross disparity, injustice, brutality, familial consequences, and social disintegration and remain complicit in their existence. There is a price to pay for inaction, and few will escape its grips. Silence is as deadly a weapon as a gun, in fact that is why so many fill the streets. The masses must react. Even more so anticipate the outcomes and act first.

The Solidarity of Old

In 1955, thousands of overworked African American men and women joined in solidarity for 381 days to boycott the legally segregated bus system in Montgomery, Alabama. It was only through the determination of a group of people who had collectively tired of discrimination and maltreatment that change was accomplished. Their fierce resoluteness, born of a growing intolerance of oppression, mounted a campaign of resistance that transcended their individual sacrifice. Recognizing the individual and collective cost of inaction and fueled by thoughtful leadership, the Black residents of Montgomery, along with some whites, faced threats, physical attacks, exhaustion and even death to accomplish their goal. The sacrifices were great and long lasting, but they persevered.

In this age of self-gratification and excessive consumerism, the challenge to galvanize a force against evil is even more challenging than before. With a majority of people lured into a state of complacency through layers of material wealth and limited degrees of success, it is difficult to hone a message of urgency. There is no collective sense of pain as there was in the past. The gradual appearance of progress for a limited few has created a false sense of accomplishment for all. It has lulled the educated and accomplished into a robotic satisfaction of mediocrity, while simultaneously masking the increased oppression of others. If only we knew the individual pain. If only those stories were told.

We all have a story

In 1991, an African American man was detained by the police in one of St. Louis' most affluent communities. He had been waiting for his wife and two daughters attending a Junior League meeting located at the time in a small, high end mall in the predominantly white town. As is typical in these racially motivated stops he had done no wrong. He had, however, paced the corridor of the mall one time too many, twice to be exact. Seeing a Black man walking in the mall gave reason to a jeweler to call the police and report a suspicious man; a Black man, of course, the only one that was there. Contrary to the report, he had not gone into the store nor even looked in that direction. So as white men walked unceremoniously in and out of the mall, there he stood, hands in the air in the presence of his wife and children being asked by the police why he was there. Later that week, his teen daughter apologized for not being with him. Inadvertently noting her father's practice of routinely having her along when he ventured into white areas of town, she had come to understand that as a Black man her father was safer from harassment or other racial attacks in the presence of a child. An incredible burden for a child to bear; an abominable indictment on the racism that still exists.

If you lived in St. Louis in 1991, you knew the story. It even made the New York Times.[187] The man who was stopped, Gerald Early, was one of the most respected literary scholars at one of the most respected universities in the country. His wife was an officer of the Junior League then housed in the building where he was stopped. As a highly respected associate professor, just as many whites as Blacks were incensed. It was certainly an event that neither he nor any of us would soon forget but eventually the media moved on. It was not until years later when reading the story in his anthology of writings on famous people from St. Louis that I learned his pain was far deeper than I thought. Though most Blacks shared in his pain, the pain was his and his alone. Humiliation, a rightful anger and a bruised ego was assumed, but I had no idea how deeply wounded he was or of the affect it had on his relationship with his daughters. The ensuing stress of the event, subsequent hate mail and confrontation with the past, in his own words "nearly wrecked my relationship with my children." Reflecting on an horrific event at his junior high school years before, Early felt compelled to dispel any notion that anyone, particularly his daughters, would summarily dismiss the fact that he had been treated like "an animal".[188] His unexpected reaction, completely out of character, reflects the deep pain, the historical humiliation and the hidden anger that every Black person carries within the recesses of their souls. It is a pain, that no amount of insight will allow those with racist views to acknowledge or even care that they have caused.

Like Gerald Early, we all have a story. If there is nothing else that you can do, tell yours. No doubt you have been the victim of crime, if nothing else the forcible theft of your tax dollars taken to support an evil system of modern slavery. Tell it. Without sharing a collective clamor of voices we become complicit in the atrocity that exists.

I have personally been the victim of every crime imaginable, and that includes the murder of my cousin's father. Even so, I maintain that prison is not the answer. The

177

eighteen year old son of one of The Ethics Project's board members was murdered in 2012, as was another board member's father a decade ago. The impact on their families continue to be immeasurable. The trajectory of each life, including the lives of the killers and their families, were changed forever. Though it had nothing to do with establishing The Ethics Project, two of my young family members have been incarcerated. One did not inform me until years later, the other, like so many, I accepted as the norm. Their minds, first altered by the streets and lack of hope and then by the system itself. Evidence that education and social status may diminish the chance of incarceration but does not fully insulate Black youth. They came from generations of college graduates, educators, architects, furniture makers and a college president. But when they woke up each day and walked into the world, the Black images they saw in the mirror became impediments they saw in the world.

Whether victim, relative or inmate, you have a story to tell; the story of a neighbor, a friend or a community. Tell your story: speak it, write it, shout it. If legislators do not hear from you, they will respond to those they do, the prison profiteers who would sooner see a child grow up without parents than loose a point on the DOW. It is not so much that they do not care what happens to that child, it is because they do. A child with a parent in prison nearly guarantees another prison bed. They are six times more likely to follow in their parent's path. If you do not vote legislators out of office, someone else will vote them in. It is your voice that will lead the way. Your voice legislators must hear.

Despite billions of dollars spent on criminal research, lectures and printed books, our culture can think of no better solution to child abuse, murder or other crimes than throwing away the key. While a pageant of pain and extinguished hope sits warehoused in prisons across America those who claim their hands are clean, close their eyes and pretend it does not exist. The state of the Black family, indeed, families of every race, continue to worsen while our democracy is taken hostage by those with ill intent. Their choice to use prison profits for their personal gain, illuminates not our democracy but our democracy's misuse. Despite overcrowded prisons and its highest ranking in the world, the U.S. continues to use prisons as its solution to crime. It seems irrelevant that such a solution comes only after a child has been murdered or a woman is raped, punishment is the only order of the day.

Print and television media sell stories and advertising based on hype not hindrance. They want sensation not solutions. Though much improved in past years, the media continue to create racial conditioning that fuels fear and perpetuates a state of racial divide. Apparently acting at the direction of racial and economic antagonists, they give a platform to those who persist in a tradition of hate and racial animosity. It is through their medium that the thoughts of society are shaped. Left unchecked, America will never realize the full potential of all who seek its dream.

Chapter 10

WHERE DO WE GO FROM HERE?

"If we feast on a diet of violence we may just become violent."

~ Martin Luther King III.

Many people can remember that feeling of separating from their mother the first day of school. They can remember in vivid detail the anguish felt after their first break up with the love of their life. For those whose father or mother took business trips, they can probably remember the knot in their stomach the first time he or she walked out the door.

With the ever increasing rate of incarcerations in the United States, more and more children are left with gaping holes in their hearts. They are left paying the price for their parent's mistake, a parent's desperate effort to support them or even worse the gross injustices in the U. S. criminal justice system that is astronomical by every measure.

The fact that one set of individuals can define what is or is not criminal and then profit from warehousing human beings in prisons might explain the injustices written about in dozens of books and thousands of articles. The fact that a group of lawmakers can decide that selling, possessing and using alcohol is legal but on the other hand selling, possessing or using even the smallest quantity of marijuana

181

will land you behind bars, is a reality in this country that has been carefully used to target specific groups of individuals and sanction the behavior of another. According to the outcomes of the mortgage collapse, one group of lawmakers decides that writing a bad check can warrant time in jail but crashing an entire economy through bogus mortgages is perfectly fine. Not a single lender was prosecuted or jailed.[189] We have witnessed a criminal justice system that allows those of substantial means to engage multiple physicians to write prescriptions for Oxycontin or Xanax without ramification while abused and neglected teens numbing their pain with marijuana are sentenced to years in jail. The practice is barbaric.

Until we demand with our votes and voices that lawmakers be fair handed and equitable in enacting laws and providing diversions we will continue to see our children spiral downward. It is imperative that we begin to protect our children, not just from drugs and gangs and shootings but from a growing system of incarcerations that has stolen their fathers and often imprisoned even them.

Prisons are no longer about keeping us safe from crime, if indeed they ever were. If safety was the concern of our lawmakers, the billions being spent nationally to keep people behind bars would be used to give them vocational training, a college education and job, before the crimes are committed. If crime was the concern, mental institutions would be the focus of improvement not closure. If safety was the concern, lawmakers would direct funding into schools instead of into prisons. Educators, however, do not walk the halls of Capital Hill making promises and selling votes. They are too busy being teachers, parents, nurses, counselors, social workers and more. So in their absence, it is the voices of those whose money does the talking that find the benefit of laws in their favor.

The approach to crime in the United States is primitive at best. With all our intellect and resources, the best we can do for someone who's addicted to drugs is to put them in a cage. The best we can do for a man who steals family is to cart him off to prison miles from his home. Further, in the 150 years since the emancipation of slaves, the United States has not evolved beyond legislating the criminalization of Black behavior. Lawmakers declare "it" illegal, like pants on the ground, then build concrete cages where fathers and brothers are corralled into sub-human existence. Like so many animals, or the property African Americans were once deemed,[190] they are branded, chained, given a number and caged. This is the plight of not just one out of ten African American men as previously predicted, but as of the most recent calculation, what is anticipated to be one out of three.[191] And for those the branding will be a permanent obstruction to voting, jobs, professional licenses and benefits.

Those who are waiting for a seminal moment to act, have missed the mark. Such a moment came when officials executed a 17 year old mentally retarded Black boy who had been abused and neglected by a crack addicted mother. There was a seminal moment when Troy Davis was executed against the pleas of even the Pope. And there was the moment when the system broke down completely, freeing a man who had brazenly killed an unarmed teenage boy. His defense allegedly paid for by ALEC. There was that moment when Amadou Diallo was killed as are many other innocent Black men killed by police.

But unlike an entire city that galvanized behind Rosa Parks when she refused to give up her seat, the media closes its eyes. A nation of Blacks rose to action when their right to vote was repeatedly denied. Dr. King traveled to Memphis to march on behalf of sanitation workers and the masses rallied behind. Yet today teenage boys, young fathers, neighbors and friends' sons and increasingly even mothers are arrested, chained together and ultimately encaged. They work for pennies a day and generate billions of dollars of revenue that goes everywhere else but Black neighborhoods. And inaction prevails.

It is time we recognize that a mindset of dividing people into criminals and "others" and distancing ourselves from those who hurt, has dramatically harmed our children, destroyed our families and wiped out entire neighborhoods. We need solutions not separation. It is time we take a stand and take back what is ours from those who see us as no more than profit in their ledgers. It is time we address the issues that cause the drug use, the gang violence and the crime with measures other than jail. It is time we turn prisons into playgrounds and profits into prayers. It is time we stop this insanity

In 2009, as the Senator from Virginia, Jim Webb, recognized that "America's criminal justice system has deteriorated to the point that it is a national disgrace," and introduced a bill to create sweeping changes. Three years later, with the bill unmoved from committee, Senator Webb chose not to run for re-election. A seemingly valiant attempt to reverse the trend of incarcerating American citizens for even minor drug offenses, the bill at least brought to the attention of many the insipid problems of a tainted system. It gave light to the practice of criminalizing and severely penalizing the use of certain drugs and the inequities in the system; choices consciously made by Congressmen while many of their friends and supporters set foot to open flood gates of marijuana and other drugs into poor and Black neighborhoods.

It was not sufficient that the drugs themselves would create addictions, deteriorate the brilliant minds of men and women foreclosed by race from the American dream, create a generation of crack addicted babies raised by crack addicted mothers, strip the dignity from hoards of men and women, induce women and men alike to sell their bodies and their children's as well, set into action a flurry of crimes that robbed families of their goods and entire communities of their freedom, and tore relationships of every kind to shreds, to add insult to injury, Congress addressed the manmade problem not with compassion and treatment, but with prisons. The original intent, indeed. The valiantly fought so called "War on Drugs" was really no more than a mass orchestrated effort to fill prison cells and fuel an economy. As prisons were built, Black men were swept up in a tornado of convictions. Those who build prisons got rich and small towns exploded. Services, restaurants, stores and housing flourished. Entire industries of services, manufacturing, and technology grew exponentially. As the census in these prison communities grew, so did allocations of federal funds. And while those communities grew, the communities targeted to fill the cells declined. Their populations decreased and so did federal funds. The meager incomes that sustained struggling

185

households were further diminished even more. Mortgages forced to be made by federal mandate were foreclosed. With each foreclosure home values declined, vacant houses were left to welcome rapes, drug sales and stolen goods. Predatory lending flourished as desperate buyers grappled for help. The spiral of decline had begun. A hideous web of unconscionable greed and destruction reared its ugly head. And so it does today.

The data will show

Recently, as Chairman of the U.S. Senate Subcommittee on the Constitution, Civil Rights and Human Rights, Senator Dick Durbin of Illinois requested data from various agencies on the School to Prison Pipeline. When all the data is gathered and tallied, undoubtedly it will show that the United States incarcerates more of its citizens than any country in the entire world; that the United States uses concrete cages to address social issues as though those captured within are just so many animals. The data will show that there are eight times more African American men under the control of the criminal justice systems than there was three decades ago. It will show the incarceration of women, indeed mothers, has increased exponentially; it will show that we struggle to educate our youth but not to lock them up. The data will show that far more is spent to keep a youth under the supervision of the juvenile justice system than it does to educate them. It will show that three times more mentally ill citizens are housed in prisons than there are in mental institutions. The data will show that we remove parents from the home and relegate remaining parents to a life of excessive work and inability to supervise or even provide emotional support to their children. It will show that prisons effectively rob the child of grandparents who are forced to step into the role of caregiver and disciplinarian. The data will show that in areas where there is a high rate of incarcerations there is a correlating high rate of disease, of mental health issues, of rape, murder, violence, child abuse, low employment, under employment, HIV-Aides and other sexually transmitted diseases. It will show food desserts, a lack of health care, predatory lending and run down homes. It will show a higher rate of foreclosures and payday loan companies lining the streets. It will show liquor stores on nearby corners and store front churches nearby. It will show high dropout rates in schools and even higher underachievement. The data will show communities that have struggled for generations to overcome racism, oppression, Jim Crow, mass discrimination and over incarceration. It will show instances of racial hatred, racial profiling and racial exclusion. And it will show over policing, over exclusion and over prosecution.

Somewhere among the data submitted there will be evidence of communities built up and systematically torn down. It will show a double standard for those that "have" who walk away from crimes with slaps on the hand and those who "have not" that are sentenced harshly for the slightest infraction. It will show children who are no long disciplined by sitting on the principal's bench but with handcuffs and police intervention. It will show school districts dismantled by forced bussing -and the money that went with it. It will show domestic violence addressed not by marriage counseling but by sentencing. It will show children begging for the attention of anyone, even if that anyone is a gang. If

187

looked at with care, the data will show why they are angry, why they cannot concentrate in school, why they resort to violence when all the adults in their lives are overwhelmed trying to circumvent the myriad of problems created by over-incarceration.

This is not rocket science. The United States continues to incarcerate, sell the unwitting public on the notion of public safety, yet watch crime increase and devastation abound. The current economic climate forecloses even the most educated and talented from obtaining meaningful employment, yet those who have been branded with a criminal record are expected to secure jobs, pay fees and restitution, support their families, pay back child support and survive off of menial or no wages. Politicians are influenced by the power of prisons-for-profit lobbyists as well as prison unions, all the while finding a tough on crime campaign a no-brainer to re-election.

Predating the existence of privatized prisons, the business of locking people in prison has long been a profitable venture. As previously stated, entire towns have sprung up and flourished via the industry. Food and clothing is purchased by the state, roads to and the prison itself must be built, jobs are created and politicians are made. The devastation to the community left behind miles away is of no consequence to those who justify the existence of prisons by labeling its inhabitants criminals. Yet Walls Street commits atrocities and gets away with murder.

Yet, while all this data exists, it is unlikely it will reflect the number of police officers who falsify evidence. The data will not likely show the number of unethical judges across the country who are complicit in the scheme to fill prison beds for payments under the table nor will it show the going price for prison stock on the New York Stock Exchange. While there are piles of data that show dismal test scores, escalation of teen pregnancies and abortions, the wide spread of HIV-Aids, it will not show the number of bored, African American teenagers wandering the streets with raging hormones, excluded from the educational system under so an Act to keep schools safe. The data will not adequately measure the tear stained pillows of hundreds of thousands of children who wake up daily to find their father or mothers gone... for years, or the number of teenage girls (and boys) who are molested and raped by the boyfriends that desperate mothers bring home to pay the bills. The data will not show their anger at a system that seems to have little money to help them but plenty to lock them up.

The data will might show the cuttings, the drug use, the bulimia and psychological damage that covers the pain of innocent children who want nothing more than to be heard. It will show how many students drop out of school and declining achievement for many who stay. It will not show, however, their brilliance, their intelligence and their dreams.

Scores of data will show that we have spent billions and billions of government dollars on "evidence based practices" that stack data on top of data, when all Johnny needed was to have someone look him in the eye –but we were too busy crunching number and looking at his pants. There is data that compares the failure of Black students to the achievement of whites; data that show Hispanics are targeted in much the same way as Blacks and that Indians and other minorities suffer injustices as well.

Most importantly, what is unlikely to be included in the myriad of papers sent to Senator Durbin and discussed in the Chambers of the Senate, is that the current state of affairs have been well calculated and executed for decades. It is rooted in the constitution and has evolved into a well-oiled machine. The real data that will be lacking, but should drive the Senate Subcommittee to act, is the reality that the 13th Amendment was crafted to create exceptions to slavery and involuntary servitude for no other reason than to perpetuate the fallen institution of slavery. But then, they are aware.

We have had data for years. Data that showed it was cheaper to send a person to college than to incarcerate them. Much cheaper when considering the full breadth of social services provided the abandoned family, than to give a person a job. We have known the injustice of the war on drugs that unjustly filtered drugs into Black communities then filled prisons with scores of drug addicted Black men and women. We knew during the war in Vietnam that if employment was denied to Black men, they would line up by the thousands to take bullets on the front lines. We have known for years if you deny them employment, business loans or office space that eventually they would find other ways to feed themselves and their families. Survival is a basic human drive. When all reasonable means of doing so are obstructed, removed and denied, man will resort to whatever is necessary to provide for himself and his family.

Any useful data must show that crafty politicians and prison profiteers label a race of people as criminals, corral them into prisons that pay them pennies on the dollar, cloak the process as a wholesome industry, keep it quiet from the masses who carry on blinded by the reality that millions of

190

men and women are snatched from their children and that families are destroyed. The data must show that hundreds of communities ravaged while other flourish at their expense. When that data is shown, the chance at reform will be real.

But we have known all this for years. This is not rocket science. The question is: what are we going to do?

Chapter 11

THE IMPLEMENTS OF BATTLE

Some are teethed on a silver spoon,
With the stars strung for a rattle,
I cut my teeth as the black racoon--
For implements of battle

~ Countee Cullen

Not another day need go by that America sits silent in a veil of disgrace. Enough of scratching our heads and trying to figure out what is wrong with Black kids. Black kids are just fine. They do not need to be poked or prodded or examined or fixed. Black kids are just fine. It is the disease of hate that permeates a certain culture bent on destroying all that is not white. When the disease is removed, Black kids will thrive.

It is time to stop spinning wheels, removing bodies downstream while culprits throw more in at the top. It is time to stop fearing the word racism and cowering if someone brings it up. Somewhere along the line we have been bullied into pretending racism does not exist and the very ones who did the bullying were busy building prisons and writing criminal laws.

It is time to roll up our sleeves, take off the gloves and do what needs to be done. Racism is alive and well and it kills all that is in its path. If America is ever to be all it can be, if it is ever going to respect the gifts, and talents and beauty and traditions that every culture brings, it is time to look racism in the face and tell it, it is time to go.

#1 DEBRIEF

For over four centuries African Americans have been traumatized both mentally and physically. Systematic methods have been used to diminish the self-worth of Black slaves and to cultivate a subservient attitude. Against all odds, millions of African Americans have transcended the horrific treatment at the hands of those who hate, and have achieved outstanding heights in the process. Despite obstacles many have excelled. Others, for various reasons, have been mired in poor self-images, lack of self-awareness, inability to elevate themselves above current circumstances and are subject to the whims of those in control. To this day they continue to accept what little is provided and believe dreams of wealth and success are beyond their reach.

Far too many Blacks have been so distracted by free wheel chairs, housing and cell phones that they fail to see that they are being robbed. Robbed of the dignity of work, robbed of the "pursuit of happiness" and robbed of savings, pensions and homes of their own. While they welcomed food stamps and vouchers their sons and husbands were whisked away to build mansions and roads, the outcome of misguided dreams born of drugs and crime. They are placated by offers of EBT cards and matchbox houses and hypnotized by fast bucks that fill prison beds. They bury their pride and true ability and accept inferior positions simply to survive. They take the bait that lures millions into a caged existence. As current leaders plead for minimum wage, groveling for the least, the narrative must change. Minimum wage should no longer be the goal. It never was and will never be enough. Minimum wage is merely enough to keep us lingering, wanting for more and pursuing unattainable dreams.

Jobs and Justice

If African Americans and others in the cross hairs of hate are to be elevated in the 21st Century, it is imperative to move beyond demand for jobs. Those brought here from Africa managed to learn trades "on the job". They learned a new language, adapted to new environments and transcended to own businesses and farms. A race of proven strength, talent and perseverance, must not be relegated to mere jobs. Always the worker, never the boss. A movement that asks collectively only for jobs presupposes an ownership of this country by those who have usurped their power. It perpetuates the notion that those currently in control are inherently entitled to and imbued with power over all. It acquiesces to unilateral control over that which is not. African Americans must simply take that which is rightfully theirs. The right to ply their trade without undue influence and obstruction. The right to share equally in the distribution of government grants and contracts. The right to engage in commerce without interference from laws designed to impede. In reality African Americans do not need to be given jobs. What is needed is obstruction to move out of the way, for those who legislate from a position of hate to be changed or removed, for those who build barriers to get out of the way. African Americans do not need anyone to hand out entitlements while others subsume the wealth, they simply need others to stop obstructing progress.

To continue asking for entitlements, government paid food, housing and utilities, dangerously perpetuates the notion of white superiority, a unnatural state of one group controlling the wealth of another. It reinforces a state of inferiority in those who serve and act only as subordinates at the direction of master. To continue along this well-worn path fails to recognize the abilities and talents of those who accept being relegated to permanent positions of workers rather than of boss. It makes complicit in a scheme of stratification those who gird the bottom rung. There is an urgent need to change the conversation and act to take that which is the natural right of every human being. Doing otherwise will unintentionally allow others to abrogate that which was never theirs.

A Name is a Name is a Name

195

Many have overheard mothers in the grocery store calling their children everything but a child of God. There are children who not only do not know their mother's real name but do not know their own. The day it became acceptable in the African American community to call each other names was the day African Americans became complicit in the plan to bring it down. Name calling is destructive. Whether young or old, no one enjoys being called a name other than the one they were given.

For the last several years I have made a concerted effort to not only avoid using labels when referring even to groups of people I have encouraged others to do the same. Inconsistent even here, but I try. During a recent voter registration effort, I encountered an attractive African American man who declined to register to vote. As he walked past he informed me that he was an ex-offender and therefore, could not vote. Appreciating his courtesy and candor, I grabbed a Vote for Me button and followed him out. His potential was glaringly obvious, and so was his pain. I asked him to do me a favor, to never refer to himself as an ex-offender again; to understand that though once convicted that should not define who he is. The appreciation in his eyes was far more than I expected. You could see years of embarrassment, regret and disappointment lift off his back. He stood just a little more erect and a light came on in his eyes. In that moment we were both elevated by those few simple word. Do not let a label define you. Period. Do not let anyone define who you are. If it is not the name your parents gave you or the one you chose for yourself, do not own it. Throw it back. Reject it. And as you do that for yourself, remember to do the same for others. If a word is anything other than someone's name, do not use it. Eliminate them from your vocabulary; from words like stupid to less than respectful words for women. Long recognized for its degrading intent, the "N" word should be by now, forgotten.

#2 KNOW THE ISSUES

If racism, classism, sexism, inequality, discrimination and disparity is going to end, it is important to identify the disease that permeates the culture and underlies them all. Until an honest look is taken at the problem that decimates African American communities and incarcerates millions, there will never be progression far from the status quo. There must be courage to see, hear and speak the truth.

For decades African Americans joined forces and demanded new laws. And with nearly every battle won, the war changed its course. After the Bakke[192] decision of the United States Supreme Court upheld college affirmative action programs that gave special consideration to certain minority applicants a new case ensued to seek its demise.[193] More recently, the voting rights won in 1965 with the Voting Rights Act, was gutted by the United States Supreme Court.[194] Hundreds of instances reflect an ongoing battle to disrupt the progress of African Americans. The "war on drugs" that actually increased the use of drugs and incarcerates millions of African Americans,[195] reckless gun laws that give the right to conceal and carry assault weapons for some but permanently eliminates the right of the millions of overly convicted Blacks from doing so,[196] are yet other acts of racial suppression.

Racism is an ugly word and the pain that accompanies it is something many would rather forget. Doing so, however, has impeded the progress that needs to be made. Trying to advance into a place of full actualization can never be accomplished with one foot melded to the past. It is necessary to move with both feet firmly planted and eyes peering ahead. We must peel back the layers of pain and look at the unvarnished truth, we have suffered tremendously, and still do. Getting to a place of realizing we were always equal, means facing the discomfort of wounds that told us we were not. Until that is done, the reality of past wrongs are destined to return.

To a large degree the hands of time have already reversed our fortunes. Thousands of African Americans who pursued degrees have incurred the debt without the job. In today's economy and even before, the Black unemployment rate is still double that of whites. The loans taken to pursue the American dream become nightmares when second hand jobs become no better than none. And consistent with laws that obstruct the road to success, even those forced into bankruptcy can no longer discharge student loan debt.[197] For many, student loans have become a permanent albatross unequalled by the weight of a well-paying job.

Embracing the Mentally Ill

Mental illness, much of which has been created by these monetary systems of injustice, must be recognized as a reality of our modern culture and addressed as the national crisis it has become. We must see the prison system for what it is, and demand that money be directed away from prisons and those with unclean hands. Funds must be redirected to counseling and treatment for trauma, mental illness and rehabilitative treatment for substance addiction. When Congress and state lawmakers hear a clamor from its constituents to stop funding prisons and start funding education and mental health issues, funding that was cut from these arenas can be restored, effectively used and increased as those who are incarcerated for non-violent offenses are released.

We spend billions to fix those things that exist only because talk of racial hatred is avoided like the plague. We continue to spin our "will" because honesty is too hard to face. But like it or not, we will never achieve true parity until we treat the disease within. We will continue to experience poverty until we acknowledge a war is going on and choose our implements of battle.

#3 KNOW THE ENEMY

It would be easy to name the enemy as those who are white but doing so would not only be inaccurate but an impediment to progress. There are as many whites who walked along side Dr. Martin Luther King, stood against bullets and bats, rode the busses and marched than there are

Blacks today taking up the cause. Too many Blacks have gotten theirs and moved on. But needless to say, there are those who remain in power, those who no longer don white sheets but put on black robes and wield gavels that are much to blame for the current state of affairs. There are those who sit in Congress and on boards across the states who are nothing more than wolves in sheep's clothing. Know them.

Hate is a disease. It needs to be treated and healed. It needs to faced head on and smoldered out. Those whose souls have been ravaged by generations of racial hatred need healing more than most. While crowds of Blacks and whites march for jobs and freedom, too many judges, police and prosecutors march to the beat of hate. They follow the dictates of cold hard cash or lures of elevation. Police are rewarded by convictions. Prosecutors have lofty dreams. Judges abandon their oath and close their eyes to justice in hope of moving up. Millions have been spent find out what is wrong with Black kids when it is not the Black kids who are broken. Left to thrive without discrimination and hate, Black kids will be just fine. It is time to stop dissecting that which was never broken and study those consumed by hate. It is time to figure out how to fix those who hate and construct strategies to heal us all.

Name Them

There are those in corporate America who continue to pay Blacks less than whites,[198] to treat others without respect and dignity. Name them. There are those who refuse to hire and mistreat those they do. Expose them. There are those who abuse their power while judging the accused. Report them.

200

Know those who oppress, name them and let them stand accountable for their deeds. For good reasons those involved in this heinous system of greed have little interest in being made known. They will pat each other on the back, hand out awards and parade around social climbers like butter would not melt. Investigate them and let them and their deeds be known.

File complaints – much is said about the misconduct of police but not enough file complaints. If the complaint is dismissed, complain to a higher authority. If the higher authority is unresponsive, complain to his/her boss. If the boss does not give satisfaction, go to the next level. *Everyone* has a boss. In the corporate world it is the stockholders - when they lose money the CEO loses all. In the government sector it is the voters, when you sway the voters you cast out the offender. EVERYONE has a boss. In the small business world it is the consumer. When they cease buying, the business does not exist. In government it is you. When you vote out those doing wrong, wrong will cease to exist.

To succeed in cleaning house at the corporate and government levels, we must be intentional. It is necessary to become informed about WHO is involved in this massive tangled web of greed, injustice, improper influence and misconduct. Despite a plethora of evidence of the ineffectiveness of prisons, the massive expenditures for ever increasing populations, the devastation wrought on thousands of communities across the country and the millions of lives destroyed, still no threat is felt by those at the top. Until *individual names* are named and each *individual* is held personally accountable for their role in this travesty of justice no one is truly safe.

The power of identifying and targeting those in control is clearly understood by ALEC. Their carefully guarded list of contributors that they refuse to disclose, is no different than the robes of the Klu Klux Klan. They hide in shame, and rightfully so. Hidden by the anonymity of white sheets, members of the Klan brazenly engaged in every brutal and illegal act imaginable. No longer assembled around burning crosses, ALEC commits its dirty deeds behind closed doors. Aided with cell phones, planes and the internet, corporate heads and legislators alike can gather in secrecy and ply their acts of greed. Any organization that can influence legislation that affects our very lives have a duty to disclose those involved. Until the pressure is on them, they will continue their dirty deeds.

Overly inclusive terms like "they and them" do more harm than good. They identify no one to feel the consequences of what is being done. Reference to "the system", "the prosecutor", "the police", "the judge" allow individuals to continue undetected. When acts of impropriety take place by police, judges, prosecutors, name them by name. Know who they are and call them out. Write to and about them. Hold them accountable for the decisions they make.

#4 CHANGE THE NARRATIVE

Fifty years after the March on Washington for Jobs and Justice, thousands once again gathered at The Lincoln Memorial to commemorate the work of Dr. Martin Luther King Jr. and the many who fought for civil rights. Fifty year after men, women and children, Blacks and whites,

Christians and Jews, were beaten and killed to secure the rights we enjoy today, leaders from around the world joined to continue a quest for the same. Thousands once again lined the Reflecting Pool and welcomed speakers from a confident, nine year old boy to Congressman John Lewis who spoke forcefully in 1963.

Speakers of every gender, race, color and religion shared their vision for a more perfect union. They recognized the progress made and lamented steps gone back. They spoke of a minimum wage which, in today's dollars, has not changed since 1963. They acknowledged a Black unemployment rate higher than even then, the increase of single parent households, and the massive rates of incarceration. We were reminded of the lack of justice and the lack jobs. As though in solidarity with those who would prefer the complaints not be heard, often the speakers' voices were muted by ill-conceived organizational choice; microphones turned off or music turned up if speakers exceeded a two minute limit. Much to the dismay of those clinging to voices of hope, inspired messages were lost by the decision of organizers too young to recognize the import of their acts. We must not be silenced, again. As John Lewis later said, "We must stand up, speak up, and get in the way."

Those on the front lines, both now and then, spoke of the injustices that continue to prevail. C.T. Vivian, Jesse Jackson, Julian Bond, Attorney General, Eric Holder and Martin Luther King III. Unlike the March fifty years before, women took the podium too; Myrlie Evers, wife of slain civil rights leader, Medgar Evers and activist in her own right, Rosalyn Brock, Chair of the NAACP and others took to the microphone and held their own. Common to all was a call for action, a demand for change and a need for unity. The long line of speakers, from ministers to youth, spoke of poverty, inadequate education, and the need for economic parity. Rev. Al Sharpton raised the issue of disrespect of women in music and everyday speech. A conversation long past due. He referenced "sagging" and the need to do more than just complain. "If we told them who they could be and what they could do, they would pull up their pants and go to work." he said. Like several others, Sharpton spoke of policies that build prisons while simultaneously dismantling schools. Others spoke of billions made by funneling guns and drugs into Black neighborhoods and from the prisons that hold those who took the bait. They spoke of the resulting violence, the Black on Black murders, the children left behind. They spoke of the long list of maladies that continue to weaken the health and strength of Black communities. In a unique moment before he spoke, I held the hand of Joseph Lowery, looked him eye to eye and was transported to his days as third president of the Southern Christian Leadership Conference. Though he went on to speak of the work past and present, just his presence was enough.

Fifty years prior, Dr. King led the March on Washington for Jobs and Freedom. Fifty years later the quest has yet to change; each remaining a deterrent in the 21st Century. While the quest for jobs is necessary, we need much more than jobs. We need businesses -capital to build them and contracts to increase them. We need to circulate dollars within the community before they exit out. We need to build wealth not simply fill jobs.

While freedom and justice remain a need, speaking it will never be enough. Though the quest for freedom is laudable, it is important to understand our own constraints; the limitations self-imposed. As Myrlie Evers noted, "we need to stand our ground." We need to know who we are, to carry ourselves with a dignity and respect that will counter the ignorance of a few. While the quest for justice is necessary, we cannot simply want it, we have to vote out those who impede it. Until we do, we will keep barking up the wrong trees and finding nothing more than unmet hope. With generations increasingly removed from the past, there is an urgent need to raise the consciousness of the youth of today. It is the young who will lead us tomorrow, if indeed they chose to lead. Leadership means sacrifice not everyone is willing to make.

We cannot rely on text books to teach the truth; text books diffuse it. We cannot rely on the media to share the voice, the media quells it. We cannot rely only on the stories told by elders, the stories die with those who were there. It is imperative to teach our own; to teach them that Gameboys are not gains, that eating in restaurants is not owning the store. We have to teach them that being able to vote is not the same as voting, that rights won in the past are empty without their exercise. They have to understand that the right to attend school is not being educated, that a degree is advancement, not success. They must understand that freedom means more than drinking from the same fountain, that it is worthless when walking-while-Black can mean dying while young. We have to teach them that building a business means building a base; that relationships are everything. As we slide back down the slippery slope of injustice, we must teach our young that marching on Washington is meaningless unless we march home and take up the torch.

In a recent report by the Sentencing Project, a number of statistics were given regarding the state of incarcerations.[199] Concurrent with reviewing the data was a webinar sharing the information by phone. In both, reference is made to the historical increases in incarcerations; a period of leveling off, a surge in increases and the current decrease in growth previously mentioned. In both instances, whether the data was being read or heard, there was a distinct bewilderment regarding the sudden and inexplicable decrease in the rate of incarceration of Black women and an increase in white.[200] Typically the reverse would be true. Even though the data breaks down the raw numbers by gender as well as by race, even including the word "racial" in its title, it fails to talk about racism, a much different creature than race. There could be any number of reasons why the word was never typed or spoken. It could be the policy of The Sentencing Project to avoid incendiary words. Racism tends to fall in that category. It could be the personal choice of the author.

What is very possible, however, is despite decades of crunching numbers, studying the issue of incarceration and seeing the gross racial disparities, as a white male who himself is imbued with privilege by the very act of being born, he simply may not see. The question mark pregnant in his voice during the webinar suggested that he truly has never considered racism and will, therefore continue running on the hamster wheel without ever looking at the truth. Racism drives the present day prison system and it has never stopped. Without acknowledging that truth, without changing that narrative, every solution considered will either fail in totality or be temporary in its success. The same is true of Dr. Chris Melde, a gifted academic and associate professor of criminology and criminal justice at Michigan

State University, who also happens to be a white male. He and his colleagues have engaged in extensive research on the impact of social interventions on youth violence, only to conclude there is no long term affect.[201] When I suggested that a continued effort to put bandages on gaping wounds repeatedly opened by disparate, over incarcerations will never yield long term results, he had to agree. Yet, since directly addressing the impact of the practices of racist driven prison industry is not one his employer or speaking audiences are likely to embrace, his work, however futile and otherwise brilliant, goes on.

In the Sentencing Project article there is a suggestion that the overall decline in incarcerations rates are "likely" due to a decrease in crime.[202] Consistent with the fact that drug courts, mentoring programs and numerous non-profit agencies who strive to reduce violence, crime and addictions are rarely given credit for decreases in crime or addiction in reports or oral presentations, the article merely references a decease without explanation. Considering the time period that the decreases occurred, between 2000 and 2010, there appears to be a correlation between the economy and the decrease. With more people being unemployed during those time periods and thus fewer economically active, fewer tax dollars were going into state and federal coffers. It would also seem that with fewer people with employment that more crimes would be committed simply to survive. What appears to be more accurate, and is supported by the articles, the changes in incarceration rates are not driven by crime but by the dollars available to pay for beds. More tax dollars more convictions. It has been noted by several researchers that even when crime was down, incarcerations were up, substantially. What gets prosecuted and when is clearly decided by the whimsy of legislators, prosecutors and judges. When the good times roll, more laws are enacted and enforced; when the money slows, policies change. The decrease in the incarceration of African American women and increase of white women can be explained from the lens of greed as well, the later represent lower maintenance. The shift in rates not only provide answers to those who clamor about the disparity in the incarceration of women but the shift also creates lower cost. With the general population of African Americans experiencing disparities in mental and physical health, it would only follow that those imprisoned would have greater health disparities as well. Treatment for diseases and mental illness would be far greater for African America women than it would be for white. African American women have more children within single parent homes, their incarceration, therefore, leaves more children to burden state systems. African American women are also paid less in the market place. All around, driven by greed and racism, the bottom line is wealth. States gradually began to experience serious budget limitations requiring limits placed on prisons. Those "crimes" that previously warranted long jail sentences for the safety of the community, suddenly were are longer crimes. Extended sentences justified by so called deterrence, no longer need to deter. By another stroke of the pen what once was crime, now is not. What once was determined an egregious act by a judge becomes a mere infraction.

From the time of the Emancipation Proclamation to the moment this book is read, incarcerations are about one singular goal, increasing the wealth of the wealthy. Until the narrative is changed and the truth becomes the conversation, everyone is simply spinning wheels.

A Rose by Any Other Name

Repeating its appearance at the top of the Most Dangerous Cities in America list, St. Louis has been consistently ranked among the most dangerous cities in the U.S., often beating out Detroit, Michigan, Camden, New Jersey and Birmingham, Alabama for over five years. The reports are denounced by The US Conference of Mayors and has raised the ire of St. Louis Mayor, Francis Slay, who noted that crime has steadily decreased in the Gateway City since 2007. Welcome news, no doubt, but not enough to close the gap between a crime rate that is four times the national average.

While the FBI, which compiles the data each year, cautioned that such reports fail to consider "numerous variables" and "over simplify" their data, there is even more reason to reject the inglorious ranking. The "crimes" being considered by CQ Press[203] in drawing its conclusions include only murder, rape, robbery, aggravated assault, burglary and auto theft. If you factor in the real crimes taking place in America, however, the rankings might shift considerably.

Politicians all over the country pass out campaign literature that amass votes by claiming to be "tough on crime". But many do little, however, about the real crimes that goes on every day in our American cities. We have been lulled into a false sense of security by legislators who advocate locking up more of our fathers, uncles, brothers and mothers for smoking marijuana, stealing cars or CD players or for physical assaults, while passing laws that allow bankers, mortgage lenders and Wall Street executives rape, rob and pillage us right out of our homes, jobs, bank deposits and dignity.

Crime statistics ignore the acts of mortgage lenders in pushing entire families from their homes after calling in loans that fraudulently concealed balloon notes in reams of paper and paragraphs of legalese. They do not factor the crimes of those who profit from the prison systems, both private and state owned or the crimes that occur within. They do not count the robbery of millions of Americans of their freedom for violations for which many whites offenders get a slap on the hand; the robbery of innocent children of one or both parents often for no reason other than self-medicating themselves with drugs that the rich obtain "legally" by bribing corrupt physicians. The statistics do not include the mass robbery of the entire world of the gifts and talents of men and women sitting behind barred cages because they could not find a job and chose theft as a means of feeding themselves and their families. They do not include the murder of those executed following wrongful convictions.

These crimes are not just as serious as rape, robbery, burglary, murder or assault, they are often contributing factors. Despite the current economic crisis created by the unfettered greed of Wall Street executives, mortgage and predatory lenders, bankers and credit card tycoons, not one person is serving time for their role in pummeling millions of people worldwide into financial desperation. None will ever be sentenced as a co-conspirator for the suicides that resulted, for the millions who have been robbed of their homes, for the robberies committed in hopes of staving off a foreclosure, for the murders that resulted in botched attempts or simply out of rage over conditions beyond their control. While some lament that states are losing money on prisons or that mortgage lenders are *currently* in a financial down turn, the CEOs and top managers who orchestrated the entire debacle have already absconded with millions in bonuses. Their mass thefts are never factored in the lists.

While petty thieves serve years behind bars at taxpayers' expense, bank executives remain free to "steal" billions of dollars from bank accounts with newly created charges. You will not see a report of the top ten cities raking in millions in tax dollars while harboring corporate thieves who helped plummet the entire economy by assessing egregious amounts of late fees, over the limit fees and excessive interest rates on credit cards. The highway robbery committed by pay-day-loan companies is not a consideration - a Missouri legislature voted for interest rates on such loans as high as 1,900% on two week old loans, and those least able to pay have turned the law into a billion dollar business.

The top ten list may indeed change if the cities like New York were cited for illegally stopping hundreds of African Americans for nothing more than driving while Black and other cities might ease their way to the top if they factored in untold professional violations by the State Court judges when stealing the law licenses of Black and solo practitioners while letting silk stocking firms "get away with murder". It is not only misleading to present crime statistics in such a restricted view of theft, murder and rape, but a disservice to all to consistently ignore both white collar crime and those committed by "boys being boys". Crime is crime and those overlooked when politically inconvenient encourages commission of more of the same.

#5 TEACH

During an annual Dr. Martin Luther King State Celebration several years ago, notable television judge and community activist, Judge Mathis gave the keynote address. It was obvious from the turn out that people were hungry for a word; that hundreds hung their hopes on Judge Mathis providing the same adroit advice that penetrates their home via the tube.

As the founder of an organization focused on the impact of incarcerations in the community, it was heartening to hear the learned judge begin quoting the staggering statistics of our prison populations. Hearing him share that African American men make up only 8%* of the U.S. population yet 60% of the prison population aroused an excited anticipation that finally someone else would publicly point a damning finger in the right direction. (*figures quoted range from 8% to 13%) Judge Mathis talked about boys with no fathers in the home (and overlooked the importance of fathers in their daughters' lives as well). It was encouraging to hear him mention how 60% of teenage boys within the criminal justice system are there because of violent crimes and that 60% of them had no father in the home. Encouraging because it seemed inevitable that the correlation was finally about to be made; there is an impact of incarcerations on Black youth. He mentioned one social ill after the other that eats through the fabric of the African American community and tears at the well-being of African American children. He referenced the drop-out rates, the poverty, the single mothers and absentee fathers. He mentioned the sudden influx of drugs and guns in the community and the discovery of the

212

role of the CIA in trading arms with the Sandinistas. He talked about drive by shootings and the cowardliness of those who shoot and run. He even talked about the prison industrial complex and the privatization of prisons. Finally someone was going to announce publicly what I had been sharing for years. Someone with strong credentials and a TV show to boot. He was on track to unveil the wicked truth of prisons -profit for some and destruction for an entire race. And then he reached the climax of his talk - the *reason* for the dismal existence of so many African Americans in every socio-economic realm. "It's the SCHOOLS!" His voice reached a crescendo with an appropriate degree of volume and disgust. "The school system is failing our children". The schools?! With his words, Judge Mathis stuck a pin in my proverbial balloon. While many inner school schools are failing to educate, they are not the cause of the failure but fail because the problems exist. The common theme of failing schools serves no other purpose than to detract from the problem at hand. The dismal existence of so many African American is a system of racism that will incarcerate before it educates.

While Black families struggle to survive in an economy that still denies Black jobs and access to capital, America's prisons are ripping them apart faster than did slavery. While schools are closed for lack of funding, more prisons are being built. While prisons funding that has increased by more than 300% the budget for education has done little more than hold its own. The problem does not lie in the failed schools, the problem lies in failed political policy.

There are millions of dollars being spent every day to bus Black children in early morning hours to school districts on the other side of town. Millions more are spent on books, computers and free lunches. New school buildings dot the entire city and more and more classrooms are led by African American teachers, many with advanced degrees. What schools may lack in physical books is readily available at the fingertip of anyone who avails themselves of the computers in both schools and public libraries. There is the Discovery Channel, The History Channel, PBS and TV 1. Students can seek tutors from local churches, the Internet and countless non-profit agencies. With such resources available, failing students, failing families and burgeoning prisons cannot be blamed on schools.

The logic behind this century old claim can be easily dispelled by the numerous accomplished African Americans that local St. Louis author , Anthony McDonald, chronicles in his book *Risen: From Jamestown to the White House*.[204] Somehow, even in the midst of discrimination, oppression, hatred and unimaginable poverty, Frederick Douglass, Mary McLeod Bethune, Ida B Wells, Henry Garnet, Madame CJ Walker, Norbert Rillieux, an engineer and inventor, George Washington Carver, Matthew Henson, an arctic explorer and Hiram Rhoades Revels, the first Black Senator to be seated in Congress, and Malcolm X to name a few, managed to circumvent ignorance and learn in the face of obstacles.

Several years ago, Readers Digest did a comparison between a public high school and a Catholic high school, no more than a few blocks away. Despite the substantial increase in spending per capita at the public school, it was the Catholic school that experienced overwhelming success with its students. The difference was not the amount of money spent on each student but other factors that often exist in families that choose to send their children to Catholic and private schools. Parental involvement was high.

To blame the current state of affairs in the African American community on the school system does a grave disservice to our children and to our community as a whole. By doing so, we ignore the real problem that permeates virtually every neighborhood, church and school. The prison system has been embraced as a profitable and politically expedient means to line the pockets of some, advance the careers of politicians who claim to be tough on crime and at the same time accomplish what was destroyed when slavery became illegal, the use of African Americans as a source of free or unconscionably cheap labor. But just as it is easier for those who profit from prisons to influence the legislature than it is for those in education, it is easier for the public to attack education than it is to attack the prisons.

The prison system routinely tears families apart leaving one parent to economically, socially and psychologically fend for the entire family and in some instances leaving children with both parents behind bars. It creates debilitating anger when injustice is rendered, it destroys the moral compass of everyone, it treats human beings like animals locked in barred cages, it leaves one out of every four African American child age 14 or older without direction, expression of love, encouragement or discipline. It robs our elders of their retirement years and of their coveted role of grandparents as they step into the role of primary care givers to "prison orphaned" grandchildren. It provides profits to those who build them, clean them, and provide food, supplies and uniforms for them. It supports entire rural communities while destroying those in the inner city. It wrenches the very lives out of many Black children who take up guns and take out their anger on each other.

Yes, inner city schools have problems, and because of that the community must be more involved in demanding curriculums that better inform Black children and more teachers who actually care. But the problem is not the school system itself but the problems it has to wrestle with day in and day out. When children enter a classroom after having been raped the night before, when they leave home with a mother shooting up, when they hear gun shots throughout the night and wonder when their turn will come, when 15 year old girls wake up in bed with grown men just to have a roof over their heads, and boys carry guns to survive, it is difficult to teach rather than assuage their many wounds. Until we stop blaming the predicament of the African American community on schools and start looking at what incarcerations are doing to those on the inside and outside of prison walls, we will continue to see the spiraling destruction of our community and the continued killing of our youth.

Teach What You Know

Regardless of your age or status in life, there is something you can teach. If you have failed, as we all do, teach what you learned from your failures. If you failed to learn from your mistakes, teach that. There is value to everything. Teach about that which was lost when segregation ended, raise consciousness of what could occur again. Teach that which was gained when segregation ended, raise consciousness of that which is taken for granted. Teach a game of baseball, basketball or darts. Sweat is good for the soul. Teach Black history, even if it is only yours. Teach how to fix a car, to sew a hem or cook a stew. Teach how to read, how to write, how to tell a yarn. Teach how to nail a board, change a light or tie a knot. Teach how to read the stars, how to plant a garden or simply how to be. Teach an old dance or the words to a song. Teach the value of time. Teach how to learn from the past, live in the present and plan for the future. Teach them how to pray, how to believe and how to be still and know that He is God.

So much has been removed from the classroom in recent year; prayer, geography, the accuracy of our past. Mant teachers spend as much time correcting students as they do in teaching them. Students simply do not learn what had been taught in the past. So much has been lost that Anthony McDonald wrote an entire book on historical African Americans to answer the questions his son continued to ask.[205] Like Anthony McDonald Jr., children are eager to know.

For years we have focused on fixing Black children when the children were never broken. We have spent billions researching, studying, analyzing and trying to fix them and yet the problem persists. We have poked and prodded, twisted and turned and yet no solution seems to stick. A disease cannot be healed by treating the wound. The site may heal but the infestation only rises once again. If, as mentioned in the introduction, the issues are not identified and addressed, the problem will never be resolved. Black children are not broken. They do not need to be fixed. The only problem with Black children are the inflictions wrought by evil intent. When removed from places of discontent, when equipped with a knowledge of self-worth, when challenged with high expectations, when loved for who they are and embraced for who they can be, Black children are just fine.

This is not to suggest that symptoms do not exist. Certainly excessive weight so prevalent among those exposed to stress and high fat foods have resulted in obesity and the maladies that come along. Certainly mental illness has evolved from abuse, neglect and systemic hate. Undoubtedly educational deficiencies arise when distractions abound. Dysfunctions result when drugs and alcohol become the food of choice. Sexually transmitted diseases abound when many Black girls seek the affection of anyone who will love them and young Black boys find value anywhere they can. Desperate for the love and affection absent from so many fatherless homes, teens follow there hormones into a den of STDs.

But Black children are not broken. They are brilliant, resourceful, talented, persistent and good. Their hearts are as precious now as they were before the world wrenched it out. They have as many dreams as those whose eyes have never witnessed death, those whose ears have never heard a gun and those whose hearts have never felt the pain of a father taken away. They have the ability to achieve as much as others if not more. They are born of resilience, strength and humanity. They come from generations of those who survived the middle passage, built a nation from the ground, endured the agony of hate and reached the Oval Office. There is nothing they cannot do.

Teach them who they are. Teach them how to become even more. Teach.

#6 INUNDATE THE MEDIA

Inundate the media with good news about youth and others. Every day electronic media is filled with reports of murders and crime. We are spoon fed a daily dose of death and destruction as though little else occurred the day before. For generations African American were made synonymous with crime. With editors and news managers choosing which crimes to report, a distinct correlation between crime and race was systematically drawn. Black images were routinely plastered across television screens and newspaper outlets across America as though crime was the exclusive parameter of African Americans. The end result proved a conscious effort to disregard the crimes committed by middle and upper class whites and target primarily those committed by Blacks of any socio-economic status. Until a change in policy was forced, each report made certain the racial make-up was clear. Indeed, on at least one occasion before demands ended such biased reporting, one local station culled national headlines to find a "Black" crime on the other side of the United States. The intent was to counter the heinous rape and murder of a two year old child by a white male. His actions had sullied the image a white purity and had to be countered by Black. To have simply reported the local news, as was customary absent a national story of local import, would have marred the image of white America as a pure and undefiled race so many consistently strive to portray. Instead, for generations the media was used to cloak "Negro" and Black men as angry, criminals, "Mexicans" as wild, sweaty, drunkards, and "Indians" as unprovoked savages. The lingering images have transcended the transition to less biased reporting and has women still clutching their purses when Black men approach, cowering in the corner of elevators when they get on and cab drivers passing by when Black men hail them down.

The media, though much improved, continues to spoon feed us doom and gloom. Today's news now includes more heart felt stories and deeds of good, but the top stories continue to be dominated by crime. As though journalists' imaginations were incapable of capturing our attention with heroic deeds of neighbors, news managers apparently insist that murders and hold-ups top the news. We are the audience. We flip on their station and purchase the products that keep them on. Without the viewers, the evening news would not exist. As millions of young American's enter those turbulent teen years, their minds must be cultivated with positive messages and images of hope. As an effort is made to turn this tide of violence and hate, it is imperative that each person do whatever they can to shape the minds, dreams and goals of our future generations. Call, email or send letters to your local news stations and papers asking for more positive reporting. Inundate the media with reports of students doing well, of a child overcoming extraordinary odds, of teachers going the extra mile and neighbors saving the day. Let them know that not only good exists in the world but it makes for much better viewing than death.

Insist that the media use its pulpit to inform viewers in a manner that protects the welfare of Americans. Reports of a murder where the suspect was himself killed is nothing more than sensationalism. It provides nothing of substance to the viewer to protect from future attacks. Coverage of a fire, while of interest to many, seldom has an impact on our day to day lives. In this 21st Century, even local news should be elevated to the level of an educated populace. The expectations mandated by those who pay the bills (those who purchase the products shown during commercial breaks) should be heightened to include information that drives our vote. Childish political campaigns showing politicians bickering like toddlers over a toy should be banned by public disgust. It is up to every viewer to take responsibility to insist on knowing that information which directly impacts their day to day lives.

Demand that the media undo the damage they created in the past. Insist that when they report crime, that they report it all. Tell the stories of corporate greed that truly affects all. Reveal the conditions of prisons that eventually release angrier men. Ask them to shape a world you want for your children by focusing on those things they want for theirs.

#7 RETURN TO THE VILLAGE

Thanks to a book written by then, First Lady Hillary Rodham Clinton, the old African proverb "It takes a village to raise a child" became a household phrase. It is one, however, that was known to many African Americans in this country long before she took pen in hand. Despite every effort to diminish the spirit and destroy the family connections of the slaves brought to the United States from Africa, the sense of village remained. Even though husbands and wives were torn apart and children were ripped from the arms of mothers to be sent to unknown parts,[206] or maybe because of it, a sense of village that came from the Mother Land transcended the separations. With the exception of few, plantations became the settings of the village mentality. Fathers were fathers to all, sometimes literally with breeding forced by slave owners, and mothers cared for whom ever needed care. Scant food was shared, and most stuck together.

The tradition transcended the plantation and could be found in neighborhoods across America. Confined by segregation, Blacks lived side by side forming cohesive communities with schools and churches right within reach. Doctors lived down the street, lawyers were right next door, the grocery store owner lived over the store and teachers across the street. People knew each other by name, they knew neighborhood children and where they went to school. They would feed a neighbor's child as quickly as they would feed their own. And they took switches to them too. Rent parties were thrown when the rent was due, hand-me-downs were passed around. One neighbor would cut another's neighbors grass. Children ran errands to the store. Neighbors talked over fences and shared a cup of sugar or an extra meal.

Desegregation opened doors to many things but it closed doors as well. Neighbors moved away and strangers moved in. Children were bussed past schools down the street, to white schools miles away. Black restaurants closed and churches were built in classier parts. Little by little that which was known as the "village" was gone. As the war on drugs began an entire new world emerged, Doors were locked, windows were barred and no one said hello. Men went to prison in record numbers leaving women to pay the rent. As more families struggled, more had to move away. A time came when people moved in and out before you knew their name. Without guidance at home children became unkempt. As they watched drug addicted parents lose respect for themselves, children lost respect for all. Gone were the days where neighbors corrected a child, told the parent and a second whipping came. As communities came to be transient depots, correcting a child meant getting cursed by the child, the child going home to tell the parent and the parent cursing you too. Neighborly corrections came to an end.

Over the years, however, systemic efforts finally destroyed the village, oddly, desegregation sealed the deal. The end of segregated housing and separate but equal schools was the final nail in the coffin of the village mentality. Neighborhoods that were once the only place Black doctors, lawyers and other professionals could live, were quickly vacated for higher grounds.[207] Lulled by more modern homes, lush surroundings and attendant prestige, those who had provided a stable base for the economic growth of Black businesses were gone.[208] Gifted Black teachers were swept into newly segregated schools and replaced with those less educated and much less concern. The working class moved further out and the youth left behind lost the images of success. Left behind in decaying streets were those who bandied from job to job, whose dreams were squelched by arrests, predatory lending, unscrupulous deals and overpriced hope.

Other cohesive neighborhoods were destroyed by intent. East St. Louis, Illinois and Mill Creek in St. Louis, Missouri.[209] Rosewood in Levy County, Florida,[210] known at The Black Wall Street and Greenwood in Tulsa, Oklahoma,[211] both two of the most successful centers of Black pride and wealth in the United States during the early 20th Century; both decimated by bombing and fires in racist riots.[212] Meacham Park, Missouri, where politicians eagerly succumbed to the prodding of big business and razed an entire community for big box stores is another where homes owned for generations by African Americans were torn down with no more concern than ink on a page, in some instances relocated and replaced with the coldness of refabricated shells. The sense of neighborhood bulldozed and tarred over in every sense of the word. Dozens of such African American communities have literally been eliminated from the American scene and with them the sense of neighborhood and the village that raised its own.

The Children Left Behind

Demonstrating the breadth of the village was the death of Whitney Houston. At the opening of the Grammy Awards show the following night, LL Cool J said it best. "Let's face it, we've had a death in the family". Of course, LL was addressing the entertainment industry present at the Grammy awards and the family he referred to was more likely than not, those in the business. But like in days gone by, on that night, Whitney Houston belonged to everyone. Reminiscent of the days when children were corrected by anyone on the block and then sent home for a second dose of pain, in our shock and loss, Whitney was the proverbial child that the village once raised. But also like the children of today, the village became so comfortable with its own success, or busy climbing the ladder, that Whitney's suffering became no more than water cooler talk. Like the millions of young men and women allowed to languish behind bars, her long and painful struggle with drugs and inner demons gained attention only when the tragic occurred. Her story is still being played out today in other people's lives. And yet, for those who were once a part of the village, the beat goes on.

The village, once a part of every African American neighborhood, the village that once filled those empty spaces left by less than able parents no longer exists. When a hole is left in a child's heart, not often enough is it filled by caring neighbors, a Sunday school class or someone else's dad. Too often it is fill by synthetic drugs and 40 ounce cans. Just Say No is easier said than done at a time when overwhelmed teachers are busier counting data than noticing a tear stained face. With a transient society that frequently sends families scattering in different directions, children are left to fend for themselves in a world filled with lewd music, immoral scripts, parents who share their weed and mothers who change men as often as they do weave. Those children, the ones Whitney left behind, are the charge of everyone. As the village that ignored Whitney's pleas and the only one that can save those still here, it is imperative to return to the village. Whitney's demons, like many before her, were silenced by her death but the pain she faced will endure in others just as long as the incredible music she left behind.

Too often when a talented, beautiful and gracious person leaves us too soon, there is a tendency to dissect their lives and speculate the reasons. For several days or even a month, as was the case with Michael Jackson, the airwaves are filled with images that depict a less than perfect life. People looked at her flaws, discussed her mistakes, criticized her choices and debated her status as the greatest vocalist ever. As with the children who pass by with sagging pants, loud music or "too much mouth", instead of extending a helping hand its more common to find the blame. The "good folk" will find the "Bobby Brown" and cast the blame somewhere else, as if all have not neglected thousands of drug addicted teens. Looking down the nose at someone else, helps avoid looking at one's own imperfect self. Making even a dent in a broken system that requires all to unite as one; a village that remembers the Whitneys who surround us every day.

#8 VOTE

For those so young that images of bombings, lynchings and a burning bus were not a part of their regular routine, it may be hard to imagine the sacrifices made to gain the right to vote. Even those who vote seemingly have failed to mandate a leadership that guarantees to all the right to the pursuit of happiness. The right to work, the right to the dignity that comes with pursuing dreams and achieving success. Comfortable with an election won, too many on The Hill, in state capitals and in local city halls have been allowed to disregard the best interest of those they represent. Those who hold both the purse strings and the power respond to either pressure or payments. If they are to respond to the best interest of the people, the people must be heard.

There are more than a few people who simply refuse to vote. They see all politicians as the same and, unfortunately what they see is not always good. No matter what argument is given to convince them otherwise, they simply will not budge. To them voting is an unnecessary evil. But regardless of the politicians who give the word crooked a new meaning, there is a reason so many fought to keep the vote to themselves. Segregationists killed, maimed and threatened anyone even attempting to register. Today their contemporaries use the Supreme Court. There must be a value they covet. Dating back to the English Parliament, white men reserved the right to vote exclusively for themselves. Even among white, Anglo-Saxon men, the vote was denied to non-property owners and of course, those who had committed crimes. Women, the young, slaves and even freed Black men all have been denied the right to choose those who would decide their fates. The violent uprisings that took place in states across the country in the 1930s until the Voting Rights Act of 1965 was passed, is evidence itself in the value of the vote. Men and women on both sides of the color line were willing to risk life and limb to prevent African Americans from voting. Indeed, the names Schwerner, Goodman and Chaney will live on in infamy as three college students, two white and one Black who were shot and buried in 1964, because of their civil rights and voting rights efforts.[213] These young men understood the value of the vote, the ability to choose those who decide the laws that governed them. They understood it as one of the most valuable rights possessed. Without its exercise those who would restrict the freedoms of African Americans, Hispanics, Native Americans, immigrants and others, will continue to do so. Without its exercise, those who enact destructive laws such as those that create prisons will continue to rule the roost.

The Power to Elect

A vote is meaningless unless exercised. President Barack Obama would never have been elected but for the millions who registered for the first time in their lives. But voting has to take place in every election not just every four years when a promising, young, African American man runs for office.

With laws that restrict a convicted person's rights to vote in most states, nearly six million people have lost the right to vote. Of those, 2.2 million votes have been removed from African Americans, 7.7% of African Americans as compared to 1.8 million convicted whites. In Florida, Kentucky and Virginia one in every five African Americans have lost the right to vote. Of significance is that a felony conviction, wrongful or otherwise, not only denies a vote to the individual convicted but removes a vote from the entire community as well. Although massive voter registration efforts in 2008 and 2012, Presidential elections resulted in the election and re-election of the country's first African American president, in local elections the loss of so many votes dilutes the power of an entire community. That is particularly true when there is a concentrated number of convictions within one community, often the case in many impoverished African American neighborhoods. According to The Sentencing Project, "[g]iven current rates of incarceration, three in ten of the next generation of black men can expect to be disenfranchised at some point in their lifetime. In states that disenfranchise ex-offenders, as many as 40% of black men may permanently lose their right to vote".[214] For those unconvinced of the importance of who is placed in office and of the impact of felony voter disenfranchisement, in 2005, Iowa Governor Vilsack, the first Democratic governor of Iowa in 30 years, issued an executive order automatically restoring the voting rights of individuals upon completion of their felony sentence. Six year later, after Vilsack chose not to run again for office, the order was immediately rescinded by Republican Governor Branstad upon his election.[215] In an era where partisan politics is divisive and obstructive to the advancement of

African Americans, immigrants and other minorities, every vote counts.

Vote for Me

In 2012, The Ethics Project started a campaign called Vote for Me. It evolved from a conversation with a young man who had served time in prison and was still unable to vote. Not more than three blocks from the Election Commission, he and I observed a group of people at the probation office who likewise were unable to vote. Frustrated with the notion that so many African Americans are still denied the right to vote after years of civil rights efforts, Vote for Me was born. He and I sat down together and designed the first button. The purpose of The Vote for Me campaign is to replace those votes lost to incarceration by having disenfranchised voters convince non-voters to vote. It returns power to those who have been convicted by encouraging them to get two people who do not otherwise vote, to register and vote on their behalf. By registering others and encouraging them to vote on every Election Day, those who have been denied their right to vote can not only replace their one vote lost to incarcerations but can actually replace them multiple times. The day Vote for Me was launched, the co-founder went home and got his sister to register. She voted "for him" in the very next election.

The Vote for Me initiative has the power to multiply the number of votes lost by state and federal laws that restrict voting rights for those who have been convicted. There is no official means of doing so, just taking whatever action necessary locally to obtain the registration form and have it returned. As with any other movement, it takes the people to pass the word.

#9 HOLD THEM ACCOUNTABLE

Hold public officials accountable. The individuals elected by the public or appointed or hired by elected officials all work for the citizens. They are paid from tax dollars and are accountable to all as citizens, taxpayers and voters. No one is exempt from the voice of the people. There is no fair political mandate that cannot or should not shift from a resounding vote of the electorate to a valiant demand for removal if not heeded. Public officials and politicians work at the will of the people. Their decisions should be a reasonable balance between the will of the people and socially responsible thought. When there is a failure of any public official to respond to that which is in the best interest of all, it is the responsibility of the citizens to demand redress or effect removal.

No matter how high the office, procedures exist to address their actions. Mayors have been recalled, judges have been removed from the bench and presidents have been impeached. A process exists to insure that those who are elected to protect the best interest of the public are held to the standards of those they serve. It is the responsibility of the electorate to assure that they do exactly that. Call, write or email your public officials. Support them on issues where they stand alone. Demand that they do what they have failed to do. Take personal responsibility to know the issues, vote and add your voice. Do not leave it to your neighbor to do. Take your neighbor along. Elected officials respond to the demands they hear. As proven by the tax dollars spent to build more jails while they close down schools, officials respond to the squeakiest wheel. Squeak.

It is important that we begin to place as much responsibility on the executive and legislative branches of government as we do on the judicial. Although judicial decisions made with reckless fiat are extremely damaging in individual cases and set precedence for others, calculated and intentional legislative and executive acts are equally far reaching. Indeed, executive orders have been used in a number of states to accelerate consideration of parole release by 60 to 90 days, thereby reducing the prison populations. Legislatures in other states have enacted changes to parole revocation procedures, thereby reducing the technical violations that would lead to prison. Taking such actions have always been within the purview of the executive and legislative branches. But, like far less educated counterparts, those whose goal is to increase profits through prison growth they have been singularly focused and destined to destroy the Constitutional guarantees of freedom and the pursuit of happiness to entire generations of Blacks, other minorities and poor whites. Too many of our spiritually depleted Congressional members, teeming with moral ineptitude, believe adherence to self-crafted articulations grant them special dispensation for evils buried within their crass decisions of racism. The plethora of laws that fly in the face of reason as prison costs go up, safety and individual wealth go down and more and more Americans of every racial background are imprisoned, supports the belief that legislators will enact virtually any law for which justification can be articulated and justification can be articulated for virtually any law. Because the overall well-being of

231

America's general populace has been disregarded for the better part of thirty years, it is imperative that we dissect the social and political constructs that allow the hidden degradation of an entire class of human beings. As more and more Americans fall within the working poor, it is time to recognize that the majority of those currently in office serve no other purpose than to support the comfort of those whose wealth and might continue to increase. It is time they go.

For those who remain, insist they hold private prison corporations accountable for breaching contract terms and filing false reports. Demand that their management be held to the same standards of criminal conduct for which they demand the public to be held. Place pressure on Congress to remove those who own or manage prisons that fail to maintain clean conditions, to protect the lives and well-being of those they contain, to control drugs from entering in. No employee or other government contractor would be retained while producing such deplorable results. No other contractors could so brazenly charge billions in return for substandard results. An employee would be fired for such failures and so should they. Write or call your congressmen and demand that failing prison corporations be fired.

Corporate Welfare

Insist that government welfare doled out to corporate interests be eliminated until golden parachutes and excessive executive compensation is stopped. Those who build massive corporations from the labor of its underpaid workers justify million dollar paychecks with the argument of their risk. But those corporations would earn nothing but for the workers who produce the products and provide the services. They could never have grown without workers who take the equivalent risk of hooking their dreams to a company that may not survive, many do not. Workers join companies to build a career. They believe their dedication will be rewarded with 401Ks that grow, with paychecks that increase or with pensions that are secure. Yet businesses close and corporations slash pay. Enron not only shuttered, but caused billions in 401K losses. The risk taken by workers are not only as valuable as those taken by CEOs, they are more so. If a company loses profits the CEO makes a million less. On the other hand, when profits are down workers lose far more.

Workers not only provide the very basis of corporate success but take as much risk as CEOs who believe their acumen should be valued more than those who do the work. While executives hoard millions in compensation and shares, they claim the pay and benefits of workers must be cut. Yet, employees remain loyal as they struggle to make ends meet. It is time those who have been forced to work two and three jobs just to pay the bills or those who make the choice to supplement inadequate pay with illegal means be protected by the government and paid fair wages and a portion of the profits. Tax breaks and government contracts should be withheld until those who toil daily for pittance are adequately paid for the work that they do. When more voices are heard in Congress, corporate welfare will end and fair treatment of workers will occur. When Congress takes measures to insure a share of the wealth for those who dedicate their lives to a robust economy, fewer people will find what has been deemed a crime a suitable alternative to survive.

Conquer and Divide

Intentionally divided by labels, U.S. citizens have permitted a government to depart from ideal principals that should have allowed an entire nation to flourish, into one that is guided by greed, self-interest and influence. Rather than look to the best interest of the country as a whole, politicians have divided us into rich and poor, Black and white, Republican and Democrat, professional and not. They label those convicted of crimes as "criminals" and make them a separate class unto themselves, ostracized and permanently condemned. Collective power is diffused by divisive words and fear is used to dilute common sense. They both distract the electorate from the real issues at hand. Though the masses will never be the 1% that control the wealth of this nation, too many jump ship in the hope that one day they just might be. They believe the hype of the economic crisis while the rich get richer off the very ones they scare.[216] Until we set aside the differences that now divide a country, collectively assume the power that rises from a common goal and hold every public official accountable for what they do, we will continue to see wealth distributed to a chosen few and the remainder missing out on the American dream.

The effect of conquer and divide and the influence of certain rap music could not have been more evident than at a funeral of a young man who had been shot. Upon entering the funeral home it became apparent that a large number of the youth attending had on T-shirts or jackets with various forms of similar letters, AFFF. As I approached the open casket, there standing just feet from the boy's father was a young man with a jacket that made the message perfectly clear, "All Family Fuk Friends". Like most from my

234

generation would have been, I was appalled. Just a few feet away from a father grieving the loss of his son, such disrespect was being displayed right over his son's casket. With so many murders among Black youth, traditional funeral attire had long since shifted from black dresses and suits to jeans and tennis shoes. Not only had no one ever taught this generation a more appropriate dress but hard times dictated they wear what they had. This brazen new message added one more layer of cultural divide.

At least half of the youth displayed one variation of the message or another. Never, from my years as an attorney in juvenile court to the thousands of youth I work with or taught, had I seen such a display of anger and distrust. It did not evolve from nowhere and I was determined to find out where and what. At the grave site I decided to ask a young man the meaning and reason for the words. With his response came the disturbing reality of what is being done to our youth. The words meant trust no one but family. Not friends and certainly not acquaintances. To add insult to injury, his girlfriend happened to see me, cut me an eye and came to escort him away. Forty years his senior, I presented her no threat. But I was certainly not family and she was having none of that. What was more disturbing than the death of yet another Black male killed before the age of 20, is a mentality that will soon create suspicion of family as well. In that moment I realized just how pervasive the evilness can run. The music being pumped into the ears of these youth, guided by an industry complicit in their demise, the poverty and quest for a job and the mere need to survive had fragmented an entire group of youth to the point where no one could be trusted and no one would trust.

What added to the irony of this funeral were three grave sites on the way. As I carefully navigated around grave markers in the ground, I crossed over three. Astonishingly they were all boys, likely all Black, all under 18 and all died on different days. Unrelated, the sheer frequency of occurrence placed them side by side. It was alarming.

With these facts in mind we must cultivate and support individuals in the community who have the presence and ability to directly address legislative bodies and public officials. Inform them of your position and educate them with facts. Do not assume they know. Frequently they do not. Accompany them to face those with the power to vote on legislative issues. Keep abreast of responses and let them know that you are aware. Engage in the political process. Whether a call made from your easy chair or walking a picket line at City Hall. Lift your voice and squeak.

#10 RESTORE AMERICA'S HISTORY

Each year across the United States, 28 days are set aside and recognized as Black History Month. Often the question arises if Black History is relevant to today's youth. Even more important is whether Black History even exists in the minds of our youth. What does it do to their self-esteem to see others so prominently featured on the pages of history books and that of African Americans omitted or reduced to a thumb nail sketch. Cautiously removed from the text of many school books across the country as being too incendiary and thoroughly whitewashed in others, the stories of countless Blacks become lost to even our own.

The full history of America is as foreign to many students as that of Ancient Greece. Indeed, those made privy to the study of world history are far more conscious of the history of Ancient Greece and other civilizations than they are about the millions of African Americans who labored under duress, those who invented modern conveniences, others who held political offices and still others whose artistic contributions shaped the very fabric of American music, art, literature, dance and theater. The obliteration of the substantial contributions African Americans have made over the course of four centuries has arguably contributed to the disrespect some of our youth display towards each other, indeed, even toward adults. The inability to see greatness in their lineage is one of the many links that explains the self-hatred and violence that continues to alter scores of young Black lives. That, added to the juxtaposition of the dominant culture's redefined image and its true historical portrait that departs so completely from reality that it has caused a malignancy to run deep through the veins of America. The image presented in numerous forms of communication is portrayed not simply contrary to the hatred and brutality that defined their relationship to Black slaves and African American citizens but is actually deified by a self-proclaimed purity. In contrast, positive images of African Americans have been historically overlooked in mass media. In later years, such images have been presented with either ringlet or bleached hair, lightened skin and culturally neutral features or broadly painted with a brush depicting violence, ignorance, poverty and crime. Valued neither as contributing members of society, or culturally competent counterparts, many African Americans became the recipients of government aid that robbed both initiative and purpose from those who grasped them as entitlements for life.

The true history of America has been lost and in its place stands the remnants of distortion and ill intent. Rising from the path of destruction and the still smoldering embers of hatred, discrimination, oppression, privilege, segregation, desegregation, Jim Crow, unemployment, incarcerations, drugs and abuse is a tainted self-image that turns inward on those who do not know they descended from an unparalleled strength. With an emphasis on educational standards that fail to measure a child's knowledge of their own history, many of our youth have lost not only a sense of their past but a sense of self as well. Without understanding the greatness and strength that flows through their veins, far too many African American youth know only the struggle they see in their immediate surroundings: the addiction, the abuse, the unemployment, the teen pregnancies, the AIDs and illness, the arrests and incarcerations. They see only dilapidated buildings and hear only destructive beats. Without a concerted effort to teach Black youth about the thousands of inventions developed by African Americans, the architecture and artistic contributions, the political strides and medical discoveries, the reality of who they are and more importantly, who they can become, is greatly thwarted.

This lack of sense of history became dramatically apparent in 2011, as I navigated the challenges of bringing an historical figure to the students in the St. Louis metropolitan area. Having lived during the turbulent 1960's, Andrew Young was a fixture in my mind as one of Dr. Martin Luther King's closest aides and confidantes. He was the image pointing toward that infamous warehouse seconds after the assassin's bullet took Dr. King's life. He was one of the men who picked up the torch and continued the struggle despite the obvious risks. But consistent with many aspects of the African American journey many of today's youth, the name of Andrew Young is largely unknown, his legacy buried with other details of the struggle for the freedom they enjoy. So who is Andrew Young?

It would be easy to explain Andrew Young according to his accomplishments. He is one of only four living confidantes of Dr. Martin Luther King Jr. who continued the cause of the 1960s Civil Rights Movement -even after standing next to Dr. King when he was shot and killed. It would be easy to list his work throughout the succeeding years including serving as U.S. Ambassador to the United Nations, United States Congressman, Mayor of Atlanta, Co-Chair of the Olympic Committee, Co-Founding Principal and Chairman of GoodWorks International, Founder and President of the Andrew Young Foundation, key strategist and negotiator during civil rights campaigns in Selma and Birmingham that led to the passage of the Civil Right Act, ordained minister, husband, father and ardent advocate for youth, but it might be easier to grasp the true picture of the man by understanding that without the work of Andrew Young and many who worked through one of the bloodiest and deadliest periods in our nation's history there would be no Barack Obama in the White House. There would be no Oprah Winfrey, Colin Powell, Condoleezza Rice, Cory Booker, no Tyler Perry or Will Smith family legacy. There would be no World Wide Technology, no Don Lemons or Soledad O'Brien. There would have been no neurosurgeon, Dr. Ben Carson or astronaut, Mae Jamison. There would be no Michael Jordan, LaBron James or Jackie Joiner Kersee. Without the work of Andrew Young and others, African

Americans would still be drinking from Colored only water fountains and sitting at the back of the bus. We would pack chicken dinners in a shoe boxes before leaving on trips because no restaurant would serve Blacks. We would stop on the side of the road to relieve ourselves and stay in ramshackled motels because others shut their doors. We would not own houses in the suburbs, or go to integrated schools. We would be admitted to "colored" only colleges and would compete only in intramural sports. We would not have worked in auto factories, city halls, or department stores – other than to operate the elevators or mop the floors. We would never have flown on planes, eaten at fine restaurants or sat on the front row of a movie theater. There would never have been an Arthur Ashe or Thurgood Marshall.

Without the sacrifice of many, African Americans would still be in segregated schools, low paying jobs and red-lined neighborhoods. Even more than it occurs, today, Blacks would be the last hired and the first fired. Chances are, much of what anyone enjoys in the country would not be but for the work of men like Andrew Young.

America's history includes a very sordid past that some have tried to obliterate to hide the atrocities of racial hatred, but it also includes the dedication of many who made possible the very lifestyles we enjoy today. There are many who forget the way things used to be and the way things have become. It is not just the younger generations who need to understand the likes of Andrew Young, who need to review American History and understand how little there would be but for the role of Blacks. We must restore our American history in the true context of how it was lived, through the blood, sweat, tears, talent and brilliance of millions of African Americans. It is important to insist that text books accurately reflect all aspects of African Americans in the development of this nation and in their treatment as well. We must remember Churchill's famous quote, "Those who fail to learn from history are doomed to repeat it." History has already proven its truth.

#11 MAKE SOME NECESSARY TROUBLE

Following the Civil Rights Movement of the 1960s many battles were won. Separate but equal was dismantled, integration was wide-spread and affirmative action opened jobs and schools. Lunch counters and water fountains were shared by all and country clubs opened their doors. So much had been denied for so long, the list of changes could fill a book. But the long and brutal battles exhausted the troops. Leaders were martyred and those who remained quieted down. So much had been gained that a time of calm eased in. Calm evolved into near silence and complacency soon set in. Student protests stopped. Hippies put on suits. Black Panthers were arrested and the other groups dissolved. Organizations have grappled with old issues that took on new forms. Segregated housing was torn down but lending dried up. Blacks were set free but one tenth were locked up. The more things change…

For decades now, efforts have been made to build on the progress made. But organizations have changed. The leadership is far removed from the struggles experienced by those in the 1950s and 1960s. Membership is far less robust, both in numbers and in commitment. Although no longer driven by the harsh reality of forced segregation, overt racism, oppression and Jim Crow, the issues of today require as much activism as those in the past. Contrasting the number of African Americans who have grasped the brass ring is an equal number who are shackled with convictions. In many ways the racial struggles of today are more damaging as in the past. Newspapers and reports across the country chronicle the myriad problems that African Americans face every day. When it comes to incarcerations, teen pregnancies, single family homes, violence, disease and moral decay, the data is far worse. The music being pumped into the hearts and minds of today's youth of every race and color continues to spawn disrespect towards women and violence towards all. Music executives not only control the artists on their payroll but through their lyrics and beats, they control the minds of youth as well. As this country continues to spiral down an economic and moral path that financially benefits a very few while destroying the lives of others, it is time to follow the immortal words of Senator John Lewis, to "make some necessary trouble."[217]

As with anything else, making some necessary trouble must begin at home. It must begin with taking responsibility for setting boundaries for children who are desperate to have them set. Too many parents lament an inability to control the music their children hear or the images they see, particularly when their children leave the house. But controlling what children listen to and what they do is not so much about what they are forced to do but what they are inspired to do. Parenting is not for wimps. It takes discipline, time, compassion, thought and sacrifice. It is not enough to provide room and board then hope that all is well. Parents are the very center of a child's being. Studies consistently show that a parent or parents are far more frequently chosen as a child's hero than anyone else.[218]

Children look up to their parents for direction and beg for limitations. They will challenge parents and other authority figures in hopes of finding boundaries that make them feel safe.[219] So making necessary trouble starts with providing boundaries and setting examples that will guide youth to make better choices on their own. It is up to parents to establish sound rules and then do as they say not as kids do.

The need for parental influence is particularly strong in a culture where more than 6,500,000 minor children have at least one parent absent from the home.[220] It is a paradox that those legislating more stringent prison terms out of the purported safety of Americans ignore that removing parents from the home, rather than providing them dignity and jobs, is actually creating a greater number of youth who are disruptive in the classroom and eventually commit crimes themselves. In the opinion of countless experts, a child is served best when both parents are actively involved in his or her life. Numerous results are shown in response to an Internet query of children needing both parents. Yet, contrary to all common sense and expert advice, those in control of incarcerating, have chosen to do just the opposite of what research bears out.[221]

There are some who attribute many of today's social problems on the lack of parenting and flippantly reply to any comment about social ills that "parents need to (fill in the blank)". However, those who do not see the community as a village and believe it is the sole responsibility of parents to raise a child, ignore the fact that a large percentage of those parents, for various reasons, are not present in their children's lives. Much of the separation between parent and child is due to incarcerations and drug addiction

243

intentionally introduced into the African American community and the mental illness the evolved from there. Those who are quick to criticize the failure of others and take no responsibility for intervening in the lives of the youth who cross their paths, fail to recognize that historically Black families have been torn apart through every generation for the last 400 years. When and how, therefore, were parents to learn how to parent? Without the example of parents in their own homes, and certainly, without parents free of addictions brought on by prior trauma, many still have no sense of what parenting is. If this onslaught of attacks on the African American community, is to be overcome, all hands are needed on deck.

Making necessary trouble outside the comfort of home may mean getting involved with one of thousands of not-for-profit organizations across the United States. With the breadth of social needs growing wider each day, there is an organization of every type to utilize the gifts any individual has to offer and to keep any individual fully engaged. From organizations that provide mentors to youth, to those teaching English to immigrants, to those working in re-entry or ministering to individuals still incarcerated, to those working for civil and human rights, there is an organization where each individual can take responsibility for changing the tide. With the Internet as the gateway to almost every non-profit in existence and public libraries that make computers and on-line access readily available, finding an organization that provides an opportunity to make some necessary trouble, is just a fingertip away.

Picketing courts and corporations that fail to recognize the value of every human being remain viable options that bring attention to issues and broadcast a level of concern. Initiating or joining a protest also connects individuals with others of like mind. Likewise, letter and phone campaigns are useful tools to express dissatisfaction with elected officials or corporate decisions. Closing a letter with a statement of intent to redirect a vote or shopping choice is an option that conveys the depth of seriousness of the concern. Those with Internet access have numerous opportunities to join or create a collective voice. Web-sites like Change.org are powerful tools for starting your own petition or to add your voice to hundreds of thousands of others to demand change. Creating an on-line presence using social media tools like Twitter or Facebook, allows you to connect with people who share a common concern or to educate people about issues of importance. There are millions of arm chair critics who can articulate a specific problem and have a plethora of solutions that wither at the end of the remote control in their hand. In today's world, every arm chair critic can become an advocate for change. It is as simple as deciding to do so.

Unite. Commit to connecting with and working with at least one other person or entity to create change. Many of the non-profit organizations mentioned below work feverishly to understand and address specific issues. Their agency heads attend conventions, participate in webinars and even write articles and books. Staffs work tirelessly to provide services and their donors scrape the bottom of the barrel to help. There are many efforts to collaborate on common goals but too often money is the driving force or the force that drives... everyone from the table. With the level of crisis seen at the hands of private prison corporations, it is time for that dynamic to change. By joining forces, with no other objective than to collectively build a coalition of organizations and individuals centered around the issue of mass incarcerations, education, mental health and other problems created by the influx of Americans caged within prison walls, sufficient trouble can be made for every individual responsible for the destruction of millions of lives. As Common Cause flexes its muscles against ALEC, other organizations must be prepared to flex theirs as well. As Change.org seeks to reach millions to demand immediate change, other organizations and individuals must respond. There is a fierce urgency to stop the attack on American citizens and that urgency is now.

#12 PUSH

Pray Until Something Happens. Prayer changes things.

Chapter 12

BY THE NUMBERS

*"Ye shall know the truth and the truth shall set you free. ...
I do not see how we will ever solve the turbulent problem of
race confronting our nation until there is an honest
confrontation with it and a willing search for the truth and
a willingness to admit the truth when we discover it."*

~ *Dr. Martin Luther King, Jr.*

The influence of those profiting from prisons has resulted in incarceration rates that should shock the conscience of any reasonable human being. In the face of our inaction, the system continues to find ways to build more prisons and fill more beds. They stop at nothing to increase their stock prices regardless of cuts in state budgets or the human toll on the most innocent victims of their plans –our children. Following is a glimpse of the impact incarcerations are having on our children, families and communities as a whole. Following is what we have allowed the United States to become.

- The United States leads the entire world in incarcerations, by far. One out of every one hundred American citizens are incarcerated

- The United States represents only 5% of the world population yet incarcerates 25% of the world's prison population
- The number of people incarcerated in America has quadrupled from 500,000 people in 1980 to 2.2 million today
- The cost of incarcerating one youth or young adult in California exceeded $200,000 annually in the 2007-08 budget year[222]
- An additional $13,000 was spent for each young adult's parole supervision in California in 2007-08
- One out of every 10 African American men are in prison or under the control of the criminal justice system. It is anticipated to increase to one in three.
- Whites are convicted of almost twice as many property crimes as African Americans and Hispanics combined, yet African Americans, Hispanics and other minorities make up 60% of those incarcerated
- One out of every three African American males are anticipated to be in prison at some point in their lives
- The United States incarcerates a larger percentage of its African American population than did South Africa at the height of apartheid[223]
- The United States incarcerates or controls more African Americans under the criminal justice system than were enslaved prior to Emancipation[224]
- 159,000 Americans are currently serving life sentences including 5300 women
- 50,000 Americans are currently serving life sentences without the possibility of parole
- 10,000 Americans serving life sentence without parole committed the crime while still juveniles

- Approximately 10,000 individuals serving life sentences committed non-violent offenses
- Revised drug laws still disproportionately impact African Americans with crack cocaine possession still being sentenced at a rate 17 times greater than for powered cocaine
- Although whites use crack cocaine five times more frequently than African Americans, African Americans are incarcerated more frequently
- Convictions reduce a person's earning potential by 40% annually, making future crimes more likely
- The average cost of incarcerating an individual is $28,893
- The United States spends over $50 billion annually on incarcerations, 1 in 15 general revenue dollars
- The rate of incarcerations in federal prisons has risen by nearly 800% since 1980
- 54 percent of inmates are parents of minor children including more than 120,000 mothers and 1.1 million fathers
- 2.7 million children have an incarcerated parent
- The number of children with a parent incarcerated has increased from 1 in 125 to 1 in 28 in just 25 years
- Children with an incarcerated parent are 23% more likely to be expelled or suspended from school
- 60% of incarcerated youth have been suspended or expelled from school
- African Americans are sentenced as severely for a drug offense as whites are for a violent offense, an average of five years

- Prisons are breeding ground for gang violence, gladiator fights, drugs, rapes, slashings and murder
- Suicides represent the largest percentage of death in prisons and juvenile detention facilities[225]
- Income for the wealthiest 3% of Americans grew by 28% between 2009 and 2011 while declining by 4% for the 93% of others
- The average wealth of the wealthy is 24 times that of less affluent Americans

Where is the outrage?

Unless otherwise noted, figures are taken from The Pew Charitable Trusts, 2010. Collateral Costs: Incarceration's Effect on Economic Mobility. Washington, DC: The Pew Charitable Trusts, The U.S. Department of Justice, Bureau of Prisons, and The Sentencing Project

CONCLUSION

The system of incarcerations in the United States has evolved into a barbaric web of greed. While America slept, ALEC and private prison corporations hijacked the United States government to create a tyranny discreetly hidden behind concrete walls. It plays shell games with facts and figures and leads this country into believing more prisons are the answer. Clearly they are not. No amount of data is needed to prove that safety now eludes us all. Those who set this system in motion continue to use scare tactics and influence to do nothing more than get rich while they destroy lives, devastate communities and leave children essentially orphaned. No amount of suicides, either inside the prisons or out, are enough to sway their conscience. It is a system of evil and nothing less. They change policies to accommodate every shift in the economy and manipulate politicians at will. There is no rhyme or reason for the decisions made other than increasing their wealth.

After experiencing an astounding level of bias and lack of ethics by the newly appointed Missouri Chief Disciplinary Council, a hearing panel and certain members of the Missouri Supreme Court seated in 2007, The Ethics Project was founded to educate the public about the professional code of conduct that exists, purportedly to assure fairness and ethics in the legal system. The lack of such ethics exhibited for years by certain police, judges and prosecutors has resulted in a prison system with a grossly disproportionate number of African Americans and

Hispanics corralled into prison cells. The majority of those imprisoned are for drug offenses that legislators change with the wind. The others often for crimes less egregious than those committed by the ones who hold the key.

That a "confederate" mentality has transcended every effort to end racism and create a safe and more inclusive society is evident throughout the United States where more effort is made to send African Americans to prison than is made to keep them in school. It is evident that not enough people embrace the talent, skills, intelligence, strength and creativity of African Americans to assure that they share equally in the wealth that centuries of their labor have created. There is evidence that too few recognize the need for a resounding mandate to end this economic and moral abuse. It is not so much those who hate that allow the problem to persist but those who cast upon "somebody" else the task of ending injustice while engrossed in their own self-interest.

One day, intelligence and decency will eventually override decades of racial hatred and oppression and those who control jobs and finances will realize that holding back another race holds back all. Even with the greatest skill of the smartest man, it is fairly difficult to advance in any great measure while having a foot on the neck of someone else.

As private prisons become more entrenched in the American way of life, it will take the collective efforts of all to place the burden of doing right in the place where it belongs, on Capitol Hill, in State Capitals and City Halls across the country. It will take voting in legislators with the tenacity to stand up to misdeeds and the foresight to build solutions that strengthen our country rather than tear it down.

ADDITIONAL READING:

1. "A Boom Behind Bars," Bloomberg Businessweek, 03-17-2011
http://act.colorofchange.org/go/2913?t=9&akid=3120.144
5768.-0OANU

2. "Gaming the System," (.pdf) Justice Policy Institute, 06-01-2011
http://act.colorofchange.org/go/2914?t=11&akid=3120.144
5768.-0OANU"

3. "1 in 3 Black Men Go To Prison? The 10 Most
Disturbing Facts About Racial Inequality in the U.S.
Criminal Justice System," AlterNet, 03-17-2012
http://act.colorofchange.org/go/2915?t=13&akid=3120.14
45768.-0OANU

4. "Private Prison Profits Skyrocket as Executives Assure
Investors of Growing Offender Population," ThinkProgress,
05-09-2013
http://act.colorofchange.org/go/2916?t=15&akid=3120.144
5768.-0OANU

5. "Banking on Bondage: Private Prisons and Mass
Incarceration," (.pdf) ACLU, 11-01-2011
http://act.colorofchange.org/go/2926?t=17&akid=3120.14
45768.-0OANU

6. "The Legacy of Chattel Slavery: Private Prisons Blur the
Line Between Real People and Real Estate With New IRS
Property Gambit," Truthout, 02-04-2013
http://act.colorofchange.ortable of
contentsg/go/2917?t=19&akid=3120.1445768.-0OANU

7. "The Dirty Thirty: Nothing to Celebrate About 30 Years
of Corrections Corporation of America," (.pdf) Grassroots
Leadership, 06-01-2013

http://act.colorofchange.org/go/2918?t=21&akid=3120.14
45768.-0OANU

8. "ACLU Lawsuit Charges Idaho Prison Officials Promote
Rampant Violence," ACLU, 03-11-2010
http://act.colorofchange.org/go/2919?t=23&akid=3120.144
5768.-0OANU

9. "Too Good to be True: Private Prisons in America,"
(.pdf) 01-01-2012
http://act.colorofchange.org/go/2921?t=25&akid=3120.144
5768.-0OANU

10. "The Color of Corporate Corrections:
Overrepresentation of People of Color in the Private
Prison Industry," Prison Legal News, 08-30-2013
http://act.colorofchange.org/go/2920?t=27&akid=3120.14
45768.-0OANU

11. "Three States Dump Major Private Prison Company in
One Month" ThinkProgress, 06-21-2013
http://act.colorofchange.org/go/2924?t=29&akid=3120.144
5768.-0OANU

12."New Hampshire Rejects All Private Prison Bids,"
ThinkProgress, 04-05-2013
http://act.colorofchange.org/go/2927?t=31&akid=3120.144
5768.-0OANU

13. "Gov. Brown's misguided private prison plan" SF
Gate, 08-28-2013
http://act.colorofchange.org/go/2925?t=33&akid=3120.14
45768.-0OANU

14."Private Prisons Found to Offer Little in Savings"
http://www.nytimes.com/2011/05/19/us/19prisons.html?pa
gewanted=all

15. "The Prison Industry in the United States: Big Business
or a New Form of Slavery?"
http://www.globalresearch.ca/the-prison-industry-in-the-
united-states-big-business-or-a-new-form-of-slavery/8289

16. "America's private prison system is a national disgrace" http://www.guardian.co.uk/commentisfree/2013/jun/13/acl u-lawsuit-east-mississippi-correctional-facility

17. "'Bargain' on Immigration Would Feed Prison Profits" http://inthesetimes.com/article/15359/bargain_on_immigrat ion_would_feed_prison_profits/

18. Private Prisons http://www.aclu.org/prisoners-rights/private-prisons

19. The Prison Industry in the United States: Big Business or a New Form of Slavery? http://www.globalresearch.ca/the-prison-industry-in-the-united-states-big-business-or-a-new-form-of-slavery/8289

RESOURCES

Following is a partial list of agencies in the United States that directly or indirectly address issues related to the impact of incarcerations.

Alternative Directions, Inc.
Michelle Kelly, Executive Director
2505 N. Charles Street
Baltimore, MD 21218
Phone: (410)-889-5072
Web: www.alternativedirectionsinc.org

American Civil Liberties Union
Susan Herman, President
125 Broad Street, (18th Floor)
New York, NY 10004

Phone: (212)-549-2500

Web: www.aclu.org

Page of Interest: voter disenfranchisement
www.aclu.org/voting-rights/voter-disfranchisement

American Friends Service Committee

Shan Cretin, General Secretary

1501 Cherry Street

Philadelphia, PA 19102

Phone: (215)-241-7104

e-mail: afscinfo@afsc.org

Web: www.afsc.org

Page of Interest: http://afsc.org/story/facts-about-mass-incarceration-people-color-us

Benedict Center

Jeanne Geraci, Executive Director

135 W. Wells Street, Suite 700

Milwaukee, WI 53203

Phone: (414)-347-1774

e-mail: jgeraci@benedictcenter.org

Web: www.benedictcenter.org

Page of Interest:
http://www.npr.org/blogs/codeswitch/2013/04/24/1788179
11/wisconsin-locks-up-more-of-its-black-men-than-any-other-state-study-finds

Black Youth Project

University of Chicago, Center for the Study of Race, Politics and Culture

5733 South University Avenue
Chicago, IL 60637
Phone: (773)-834-1706
e-mail: info@blackyouthproject.com
Web: www.blackyouthproject.com

Brennan Center for Justice at New York University School of Law
Michael Waldman, President
161 Avenue of the Americas, (12th Floor)
New York, NY 10013
Phone: (646)-292-8310
e-mail: brennancenter@nyu.edu
Web: www.brennancenter.org

Broken on All Aides (documentary)
Matthew Pillische Director
e-mail: brokenonallsides@gmail.com
Web: www.brokenonallsides.com

Campaign to End the New Jim Crow
490 Riverside Drive
New York, NY 10027
Phone: (212)-501-2112
Web: www.endnewjimcrow.org

Center for Community Alternatives: Innovative Solutions for Justice
Marsha Weissman Executive Director

115 E. Jefferson Street, Suite 300
Syracuse, NY 13203
Phone: (315)-422-5638
e-mail: mweissman@communityalternatives.org
Web: www.communityalternatives.org

Center for Constitutional Rights
Vincent Warren, Executive Director
666 Broadway, (7th floor)
New York, NY 10012
Phone: (212)-614-6464
Web: www.ccrjustice.org

The Center for Prisoner Health and Human Rights
Bradley W. Brockmann, Executive Director
8 Third Street, (2nd Floor)
Providence, RI 0206
Phone: (401)-793-4783
email: bbrockmann@lifespan.org
Web: www.brown.edu/Research/Prisonerhealth

Center for the Study of Civil and Human Rights Law
Van Henri White, Founder
18 Grove Place, Rochester, New York 14605.
Phone: (585) 271-6780
e-mail: van.white@thelegalbrief.com.
Web-site: www.thelegalbrief.com

College Initiative
Michael Carey, Executive Director
29-76 Northern Boulevard
Long Island, NY 11101
Phone: (347)-669-2864
e-mail: info@collegeinitiative.org
Web: www.collegeinitiative.org

Correctional Association of New York
Soffiyah Elijah, Executive Director
2090 Adam Clayton Powell Blvd., Suite 200
New York, NY 10027
Phone: (212)-254-5700
Web: www.correctionalassociation.org

Critical Resistance
1904 Franklin Street, Suite 504
Oakland, CA 94612
Phone: (510)-444-0484
e-mail: crnational@criticalresistance.org
Web: www.criticalresistance.org

Ella Baker Center for Human Rights
Jakada Imani, Executive Director
1970 Broadway, Suite 450
Oakland, CA 94612
Phone: (510)-428-3939
Web: www.ellabakercenter.org

Page of Interest: Books not Bars:
http://ellabakercenter.org/our-work/books-not-bars

Equal Justice Initiative
Bryan Stevenson, Founder/ Executive Director
122 Commerce Street
Montgomery, AL 36104
Phone: (334)-269-1803
e-mail: contact_us@eji.org
Web: www.eji.org
Page of interest: TED talk given by EJI director,
http://www.ted.com/talks/bryan_stevenson_we_need_to_t
alk_about_an_injustice.html

Families Against Mandatory Minimums
Julie Stewart
President, Founder
1100 H Street NW, Suite 1000
Washington, DC 20005
Phone: (202) 822-6700
e-mail: famm@famm.org
Web: www.famm.org

**Family and Friends of Louisiana's Incarcerated
Children**
Gina Womack, Executive Director
1600 Oretha C. Haley Blvd.
New Orleans, LA 70113
Phone: (504)-522-5437
e-mail: gbwomack@fflic.org

Web: www.fflic.org

FedCURE
P.O. Box 15667
Plantation, FL 33318-5667
Fax: 801-672-7777
Web: www.fedcure.org

The Fortune Society
29-76 Northern Blvd.
Long Island City, NY 11101
Phone: (212)-691-7554
Web: www.fortunesociety.org

Goodwill Industries International
15810 Indianola Drive
Rockville, MD 20855
Phone: (800)-466-39455
e-mail: contactus@goodwill.org
Web: www.goodwill.org
Page of Interest: http://www.goodwill.org/my-story/cornelius-furr/

Grassroots Leadership
Bob Libal, Executive Director
1346 St. Julien Street
Charlotte, NC 28205
Phone: (512)-971-0487
e-mail: blibal@grassrootsleadership.org

Web: www.grassrootsleadership.org

HG.org Global Legal Resources
Web: www.hg.org

Hour Children
Sister Tesa Fitzgerald, Executive Director
13-07 37th Avenue
New York, NY 11101
Phone: (718)-433-4724
e-mail: sistertesa@hourchildren.org
Web: www.hourchildren.org

Human Rights Watch
Kenneth Roth, Executive Director
350 Fifth Avenue, (34th floor)
New York, NY 10118-3299
Phone: (212)-290-4700
Web: www.hrw.org
Page of Interest: www.hrw.org/news/2013/01/31/us-injustices-filling-prisons

Innocence Project
Barry C. Scheck and Peter J. Neufeld, Co-Directors
40 Worth Street, Suite 701
New York, NY 10013
Phone: (212)-364-5340
e-mail: info@innocenceproject.org
Web: www.innocenceproject.org

Justice Policy Initiative
Tracy Velázquez, Executive Director
1012 14th Street, NW Suite 400
Washington, DC 2005
Phone: (202)-558-7974
e-mail: tracy@justicepolicy.org
Web: www.justicepolicy.org

Juvenile Law Center
Robert Schwartz, Executive Director
The Philadelphia Building, 1315 Walnut Street, (4th Fl)
Philadelphia, PA 19107
Phone: (215)-625-0551
Web: www.jlc.org
Page of interest: http://www.jlc.org/calendar/2012-
03/trainings-and-presentations/racial-injustice-school-
prison-pipeline-and-disproporti

The Leadership Conference on Civil & Human Rights
Wade Henderson. President, CEO
1629 K Street, NW (10th floor)
Washington, DC 20006
Phone: (202)-466-3311
Web: www.civilrights.org/publications/justice-on-
trial/consequences.html

NAACP
Roslyn Brock. Chairwoman

4805 Mt. Hope Drive
Baltimore, MD 21215-3297
Phone: (410)-580-5777
Web: www.naacp.org/pages/misplaced-priorities

National Council on Crime and Delinquency
Alex Busansky, President
1970 Broadway, Suite 500
Oakland, CA 94612
Phone: (800)-306-6223
e-mail: info@nccdglobal.org
Web: www.nccdglobal.org

Office of the Appellate Defender
Anastasia Heeger
Director of Reinvestigation Project
1 Park Place, Suite 1601
New York, NY 10007
Phone: (212)-402-4100
e-mail: aheeger@appellatedefender.org
Web: www.appellatedefender.org

The Osborne Association
Elizabeth Gaynes, Executive Director
809 Westchester Avenue
Bronx, NY 10455
Phone: (718)-707-2600
Web: www.osborneny.org

Penal Reform International
60-62 Commercial Street
London, E1 6LT
United Kingdom
Phone: +44-20-7247-6515
e-mail: info@penalreform.org
Web: www.penalreform.org

Prison Activist Resource Center
P.O. Box 70447
Oakland, CA 94612
Phone: (510)-893-4648
e-mail: prisonactivist@gmail.com
Web: www.prisonactivist.org

Prison Outreach Ministry, Inc.
Sister Susan Van Baalen, Executive Director
P.O. Box 4597
Washington DC, 20017
Phone: (202)-772-4300
e-mail: svanbaalen@prisonoutreachministry.org
Web: www.prisonoutreachministry.org

Prison Policy Initiative
Peter Wagner, Executive Director
P.O. Box 127
Web: www.prisonpolicy.org
Page of Interest: http://www.prisonersofthecensus.org,

http://www.wmitchell.edu/lawreview/Volume38/docume nts/2.Wagner.pdf

Public Welfare Foundation
Mary McClymont. President
1200 U Street, NW
Washington DC, 20009-4443
Phone: (202)-965-1800
e-mail: info@publicwelfare.org
Web: www.publicwelfare.org

Reentry.net
Web: www.reentry.net

Rock the Vote
Heather Smith. President
1001 Connecticut Ave., NW Suite 640
Washington DC, 20036
Phone: (202)-719-9910
Web: www.rockthevote.com
Page of Interest: voting as a felon
http://www.rockthevote.com/election-center/voting-ex-felon/

Russell Sage Foundation
Eric Wanner
President, Founder
112 East 64th Street
New York, NY 10065

Phone: (212)-750-6000
Web: www.russellsage.org

The Sentencing Project
Marc Mauer. Executive Director
1705 DeSales Street, NW (8th floor)
Washington DC, 20036
Phone: (202)-628-0871
e-mail: staff@sentencingproject.org
Web: www.sentencingproject.org

Services to Children and Families of Prisoners
U.S. Department of Health and Human Services
e-mail: info@childwelfare.gov
Web: www.childwelfare.gov

The Stop Mass Incarceration Network
P.O. Box 941, Knickerbocker Station
New York, NY 1002-0900
Phone: (347)-979-7646
e-mail: stopmassincarceration@gmail.com
Web: www.stopmassincarceration.org
Page of Interest: Bare Witness Project
www.bearwitnessproject.tumblr.com

Students Against Mass Incarceration
Web: www.sami-national.org

The Ethics Project
Christi Griffin, Founder & President
40 N. Kingshighway, 12F
St. Louis, MO 63108
Phone: 314-495-9528
email: theethicsproject@gmail.com
Web: www.TheEthicsProject.org

Think Outside the Cell Foundation
Shelia Rule. Founder
511 Avenue of the Americas, Suite 525
New York, NY 10011
Phone: (877)-267-2303
e-mail: thinkoutsidethecell@verizon.net
Web: www.thinkoutsidethecell.org

U.S. Department of Justice: Office of Justice Programs
810 Seventh Street, NW
Washington DC, 20531
Phone: (202)-307-0703
e-mail: askojp@ncjrs.gov
Web: www.ojp.usdoj.gov

Urban Justice Center's Human Rights Project
Shani Jamila. Director
123 William Street, (16th Floor)
New York, NY 10038
Phone: (646)602-5600
Web: www.hrpujc.org

Vera Institute of Justice
Karen Goldstein
Interim Director, Vice President and General Counsel
233 Broadway, (12th Floor)
New York, NY 10279
Phone: (212)-376-3144
e-mail: kgoldstein@vera.org
Web: www.vera.org

Washington Lawyers' Committee of Civil Rights and Urban Affairs
Roderic Boggs. Executive Director
11 Dupont Circle, NW Suite 400
Washington DC, 20036
Phone: (202)-319-1000
e-mail: rod_boggs@washlaw.org
Web: www.washlaw.org

William Moses Kunstler Fund for Racial Justice
13 Gay Street
New York, NY 10014
Phone: (212)-924-6980
e-mail: info@kunstler.org
Web: www.kunstler.org

Women's Prison Association
Georgia Lerner
Executive Director
110 Second Avenue

New York, NY 10003
Pone: (646)-292-7740
email: glerner@wpaonline.org
Web: www.wpaonline.org

Private Prison & Related Corporations

Following is a list of corporations directly or indirectly sharing in the profits derived from prisons. Identifying individuals who profit from this modern form of slavery was daunting. The list is not exhaustive.

1. Federal Prison Industries (FPI, UNICOR)

www.unicor.gov
320 First Street
Washington D.C. 20534

2. Corrections Corporation of America

www.cca.com
10 Burton Hills Boulevard
Nashville, TN 37215
Phone: (615) 263-3000, (800) 624-2931
Fax: (615) 263-3140

3. American Correctional Association

www.aca.org
206 North Washington Street. Suite 200
Alexandria, VA 22314
Phone: (800) 222-5646

4. Corizon- Prison Health Management

www.corizonhealth.com

Corizon Headquarters

105 Westpark Dr Ste 200
Brentwood, TN 37027

Corizon Operational Headquarters

12647 Olive Blvd
St Louis, MO 63141

5. Wexford Health

www.wexfordhealth.com

425 Holiday Drive, Foster Plaza Two
Pittsburgh, PA 15220

Phone: (888) 633-6468
Fax: (412) 937-8599
E-mail: info@wexfordhealth.com

6. National Commission on Correctional Health Care

www.ncchc.org

1145 W. Diversey Pkwy.
Chicago, IL 60614

Phone: (773) 880-1460
Fax: (773) 880-2424
Email: info@ncchc.org

7. The GEO Group, Inc.

www.geogroup.com

One Park Place

Incarcerations in Black and White

621 NW 53rd Street, Suite 700
Boca Raton, FL 33487

8. Transcor
www.transcor.com
646 Melrose Avenue
Nashville, TN 37211-2161
Phone: (615) 251-7008
transcorinfo@transcor.com

9. Haines & Kibblehouse
www.hkgroup.com
P.O. Box 196
2052 Lucon Road
Skippack, PA 19474
Phone: (610) 584-8500

10. Cornerstone Detention Products Inc.
www.cornerstonedetention.com
Cornerstone Detention Products, Inc.

25270 Will McComb Drive
Tanner, AL 35671
Phone: (256) 355-2396
Fax: (256) 560-4284
Email: info@CornerstoneDetention.com

Cornerstone Institutional, LLC

25270 Will McComb Drive
Tanner, AL 35671
Phone: (877)-298-7351
Fax: (256) 560-4284
Email: slclaborn@CornerstoneDetention.com

11. Detention Equipment Manufacturers Association (DEMA)

www.naamm.org

800 Roosevelt Rd. Bldg. C, Suite 312
Glen Ellyn, IL 60137
Voice: 630-942-6591 / Fax: 630-790-3095

12. American Jail Products

www.americanjailproducts.com

4 Van Buren Street
Troy, New York 12180

Phone: (518) 271-6560
Fax: (518) 266-1243
Email: george@americanjailproducts.com

13. Southern Folger Detention Equipment Company

www.southernfolger.com

4634 S. Presa St.

San Antonio, TX 78223-1058

Phone: (210) 533-1231

Fax: (210) 533-2211

14. ARAMARK

www.aramark.com, www.aramarkcorrections.com

1101 Market Street

Philadelphia, PA 19107

Phone: (800) 777-7090

Email info@aramarkcorrections.com

15. Scopia Capital Management LLC
www.scopiacapital.com
152 West 57th Street, 33rd Floor
New York, NY 10019
Phone: (212) 370-0303
Fax: (212) 370-0404

16. Fidelity Investments
www.fidelity.com
Boston, MA

17. The Vanguard Group
www.vanguard.com
P.O. Box 2600€€
Valley Forge, PA 19482

18. ALEC – The American Legislative Exchange Council
www.ALEC.org
2900 Crystal Drive, 6th Floor
Arlington, VA 22202
Phone: 703-373-0933

The following is a list of Corporate ALEC members as of 2013, as listed on the web-site of Common Cause, a nonpartisan, nonprofit advocacy organization founded in 1970, "as a vehicle for citizens to make their voices heard in the political process and to hold their elected leaders accountable to the public interest."[226] According to Common Cause, its mission is to "strengthen our

274

democracy by empowering our members, supporters and the general public to take action on critical policy issues."[227] It is committed to honest, open and accountable government, as well as encouraging citizen participation in democracy."[228]

LogistiCare Solutions, LLC, Macquarie Capital USAMarathon Oil Company, MDU Resources Group, Inc.,MedImmune, Company of AstraZeneca, Merck & Company, Inc, Microsoft Corporation, VeriSol, National Federation of Independent Business (NFIB), National Heritage Academies, Naational Taxpayers Union, Norfolk Southern Corporation, Novartis Corporation, Energy, Inc.,Occidental Oil & Gas Co.Occidental Petroleum Corporation, Orchid Cellmark PacifiCorp, Parquet Public Affairs, Peabody Energy, Pfizer Inc., Philip Morris International, Pinnacle West Capital Corp. Publix Super Markets, Inc., Purdue Pharma L.P., Qwest Communications International Inc., RAI Services Company ResCare, Reynolds American Inc., International/Federal Relations; Rubber Manufacturers Association, Salt River Project, Sanofi-Aventis, SAP America, Inc., Security Finance Corporation, Shell Oil Company, Shook, Hardy & Bacon, L.L.P., State Farm Insurance Companies, T-Mobile USA, Pharmaceuticals North America Inc.,   TASER International, TEVA Pharmaceuticals, Texas Roadhouse, The DIRECTV Group, Inc., The Doctors Management Company, Time Warner Cable, Communications & Technology Transurban, U.S. Chamber Institute for Legal Reform, United Parcel Service, UnitedHealth Group, US Oncology, Verizon Communications, VISA U.S.A. Inc., WellPoint, Inc., Wine Institute, Wise Carter Child & Caraway, Yahoo! Inc.,
-

According to the same report the following corporations have left ALEC. This list was current as of July 26, 2012.

275

Amazon.com, American Traffic Solutions, Amgen Inc., Arizona Public Service, Best Buy, Blue Cross Blue Shield, Coca-Cola Company, Connections Academy, CVS Caremark, Dell Computers, EnergySolutions, Entergy, Express Scripts, General Electric, General Motors, Hewlett-Packard, Intuit, John Deere & Company, Johnson & Johnson, Kaplan, Kraft, Louis Dreyfus, Mars, McDonald's, Medco, Medtronic, MillerCoors, Pepsi, Procter & Gamble, Reckitt Benckiser Group, Reed Elsevier, Scantron Corporation, Sprint Nextel, Symantec, YUM! Brands, Walgreens,Wal-Mart, Wendy's, Western Union (Non-Profits) Gates Foundation, Lumina Foundation for Education, National Board for Professional Teaching Standards, National Association of Charter School Authorizers

The following are United States Senators who serve as the National Chairs of ALEC:
Rep. John Piscopo, Nat'l Chair, CT, Rep. Linda Upmeyer, 1st V Chair, IA, Rep. Phil King, 2nd Vice Chair, TX, Sen. Leah Vukmir, Treasurer, WI, Rep. Liston Barfield, Secretary, SC, Rep. David Frizzell, Immediate Past Chair, IN, Chair Emeritus, Rep. Harold Brubaker, NC, Rep. Tom Craddick,TX, Rep. Noble Ellington, LA, Sen. Steve Faris, AK, Rep. Bobby Hogue, AK, Sen. Owen Johnson, NY, Rep. Dolores Mertz, IA, Board Members, Rep. Gary Banz, OK, Sen. Jim Buck, IN, Sen. Bill Cadman, CO, Sen. Barbara Cegavske, NV, Rep. Joe Harrison, LA, Speaker Bill Howell, VA, Sen. Michael Lamoureux, AK,Rep. Steve McDaniel, TN, Speaker Ray Merrick, KS, Sen. Wayne Niederhauser, UT, Speaker Thom Tillis, NC, Rep. Curry Todd, TN, Sen. Susan Wagle, KS, Rep. Blair Thoreson, ND, Rep. Tim Moffitt, NC, Sen. Bill Seitz, OH, F. William McNabb III, Chair & CEO, Emerson U. Fullwood, boardmber, Rajiv.Gupta, board member, Amy Gutmann,

* Though the neighbor and his attorney had called my office repeatedly for a week feigning an interest in closing on the house, once all issues were resolved, ample evidence proved the calls were no more than a ruse. After I filed a Ch. 13 bankruptcy proposing a plan to stop the foreclosure and sell the house to the neighbor, his attorney filed a Motion in Opposition citing more than 25 reasons why the court should not permit the sale.

**Having no real estate investment experience and insufficient funds to pay off the entire mortgage, I enlisted a friend to help pay off the mortgage. He was also party to the secondary contract that was drafted by another law firm with only hours to spare before the scheduled foreclosure.

***Judge Ronnie White recused himself from the Mo Supreme Court hearing and did not participate in my suspension. Judge George Draper had not been appointed to the bench.

BIBLIOGRAPHY

[1] Joy DeGruy Leary, *Post Traumatic Slave Syndrome,* (Milwaukie, Uptone Press, 2005), pg 54

[2] Leon Festinger, Henry W. Riecken, Stanley Schachter, *When Prophecy Fails* Minneapolis, University of Minnesota Press, 1956

[3] Michelle Alexander, *The New Jim Crow: Mass Incarceration in the Age of Colorblindness,* New York, The New Press, 2010

[4] Council on Foreign Relations, "U.S. Education Slipping in Ranks Worldwide, Earns Poor Grades on CFR Scorecard", Jun 17, 2013

[5] Amrutha Gayathri, "US 17th In Global Education Ranking; Finland, South Korea Claim Top Spots", International Business Times, Nov 27, 2012

[6] Wal Mart Stores, Inc. v Dukes, et al, United State Supreme Court slip opinion, No. 10–277. Decided Jun 20, 2011

[7] Lila Shapiro, "Walmart: Too Big to Sue", Huffington Post, Jun 20, 2011

[8] Saul S. Friedman *Jews and the American Slave Trade*, New Brunswick, Transaction Publishers, Jan 4, 1999

[9] Chris Edwards, "Indian Lands, Indian Subsidies, and the Bureau of Indian Affairs", Cato Institute, Downsizing the Federal Government, Feb 2012

[10] Dale Gieringer, "125th Anniversary of the First U.S. Anti-Drug Law: San Francisco's Opium Den Ordinance", drugsense.org, Nov 15, 1875

[11] Seth Cagin, Phillip Dray, *We Are Not Afraid: The Story of Goodman, Schwerner and Chaney, and the Civil Rights Campaign for Mississippi,* New York, Nation Books, 2006

[12] Amy L. Koehlinger, *The New Nuns: Racial Justice and Religious Reform in the 1960s,* Cambridge, Harvard University Press, Apr 30, 2007

[13] Nadra Kareem Nittle, "Race, Intolerance and the Church", Race Relations, About.com, undated

[14] A. Leon Higginbotham, Jr. *Shades of Freedom,* New York, Oxford University Press, New York, 1996, pg 46

[15] Isabel Wilkerson, *The Warmth of Other Suns,* New York, Random House, 2010, pg 39

[16] Douglas A. Blackmon, Ibid, pg 44

[17] Joy DeGruy Leary, Ibid, pgs 77-82

[18] Ann Kellan, "Bones reveal little-known tale of New York slaves", CNN,com, Feb 12, 1998

[19] Joy DeGruy Leary, Ibid, 73

[20] Marie Diamond, "Tennessee Tea Party 'Demands' That References To Slavery Be Removed From History Textbooks", ThinkProgressive.org, Jan. 23, 2012

[21] Lawrence G. Duggan, "Indulgence", Encyclopedia Britannica

[22] Kenneth M. Stamp, *The Peculiar Institution, Slavery in the Ante Bellum South,* New York, Vintage Books, 1989

[23] Ibid, 64

[24] Joel Dyer, *The Perpetual Prisoner Machine: How America Profits from Crime,* Aurora, Westview Press, 2008, pg 55

[25] Ibid, pg 55

[26] Steven D. Levitt , "Understanding Why Crime Fell in the 1990s: Four Factors that Explain the Decline and Six that Do Not", Journal of Economic Perspectives—Volume 18, Number 1—Winter 2004—Pgs 163–190

[27] Citizens United v Federal Election Commission, United States Supreme Court slip opinion, No. 08–205. Jan 21, 2010

[28] Douglas A. Blackmon, *Slavery by Another Name: The Re-Enslavement of Black Americans from the Civil War to World War II,* New York, Doubleday, 2008, pg 90-99

[29] Ibid, pg 99

[30] Joy Degruy Leary, Ibid, pg 85

[31] The Thirteenth Amendment of the United States Constitution, 1865

[32] Douglas Blackmon, Ibid, 55

[33] Douglas Blackmon, 53-56

[34] Tracey Kyckelhahn, State Corrections Expenditures, FY 1982-2010 U.S. Department of Justice, Office of Justice Programs, Bureau of Justice Statistics, BJS Bulletin, NCJ 239672 Dec., 2012

[35] Annual Financial Statements Fiscal Year 2011, U.S. Department of Justice, Office of the Inspector General, Audit Division, Audit Report 12-09, Jan.,2012

[36] Justice Police Institute, "Maryland Almost Maxes Out Prisons in 2010, Increases Prison Population Nearly Two Percent", Dec 15, 2011

[37] National Association for the Advancement of Colored People, *Criminal Justice Fact Sheet,* 2009-2013

[38] National Association for the Advancement of Colored People, *ibid*

[39] The National Journal, Millions of Felons Barred from Voting Booth by Rosa Ramirez, July 17, 2012.

[40] Ibid

[41] Fair Sentencing Act of 2010, 21 USC 801, Enacted Aug 3, 2010

[42] Tracey L. Shollenberger, "Racial Disparities in School Suspension and Subsequent Outcomes: Evidence from the National Longitudinal Survey of Youth 1997", The Civil Rights Project, UCLA, Apr 6, 2013

[43] Sudhin Thanawala, "Deshon Marman Saggy Pants Arrest: No Charges In SF Airport Case" Huffington Post San Francisco", Jul. 13, 2011

[44] Tony Newman, Anthony Papa, "Former NYPD Detective Testifies that Police Regularly Plant Drugs on Innocent People to Meet Arrest Quota", Drug Policy Alliance, Oct 13, 2011

[45] Sudhin Thanawala, Ibid

[46] Abby Goodnough, "Harvard Professor Jailed; Officer Is Accused of Bias" The New York Times, July 20, 2009

[47] Michael Cooper, "Officers in Bronx Fire 41 Shots, And an Unarmed Man Is Killed", The New York Time, Feb 05, 1999

[48] The United States Constitution, 13th Amendment, Article II, 1865

[49] Douglas A. Blackmon, Ibid pgs 53, 54

[50] Ibid

[51] Lutz Kaelber, Presentation Eugenics: Compulsory Sterilization in 50 American States, University of Vermont, 2012

[52] Lutz Kaelber, Ibid

[53] Ashley Nellis, Ph.D. with research assistance provided by Katherine Zafft and Cody Mason, "The Lives of Juvenile Lifers: Findings from a National Survey", The Sentencing Project, March, 2012

[54] Institute on Women and Criminal Justice, Quick Facts: Women & Criminal Justice – 2009

[55] The Adoption and Safe Families Act (ASFA, Public Law 105-89) Nov 19, 1997

[56] Incarcerated Parents and Their Children: Trends 1991-2007, Sarah Schirmer, Ashley Nellis, and Marc Mauer, The Sentencing Project, February, 2009, pg 9

[57] R. Neil Siler, *How I Go Over: Healing from the African American Soul,* Virginia, New Life Publishing, 2010, pg. 30

[58] Christopher Wildeman, Yale University, "Children of Imprisoned Parents – Unintended Casualties of The Prison Boom", Scholars Strategy Network, April, 2011

[59] Ashley Nellis, and Marc Mauer, Ibid, pg 4

[60] Ibid, 4

[61] Ibid, 3

[62] James Austin, Ph.D., Garry Coventry, Ph.D, "Emerging Issues on Privatized Prisons", Bureau of Justice Assistance, Monograph NCJ 181249, Feb, 2001

[63] Federal Bureau of Prison, U.S. Depart. of Justice "Work Programs", 2013

[64] Mission Statement, The Innocence Project, www.TheInnocenceProject.org, 2013

[65] The Sentencing Project, Life Goes on: The Historic Rise in Life Sentences in America, Sept 27, 2013

[66] "Juvenile Law without Parole", Center for Children's Law and Policy, undated, citing Amnesty International and Human Rights Watch,

[67] U. S. Supreme Court: Roper v. Simmons, No. 03-633, Mar 1, 2005

[68] Graham v Florida, U.S. Supreme Court, No. 08–7412, May 17, 2010

[69] Miller v. Alabama, No-10-9646 and Jackson v. Hobbs, U.S. Supreme Court, No. 10-9647, Jun 25, 2010

[70] Ashley Nellie, PhD, with research assistance from Jean Chung, "Life Goes On: The Historic Rise in Life Sentences in America, The Sentencing Project, 2013

[71] Ibid, pg 1

[72] "Annual Determination of Average Cost of Incarceration", A Notice by the Prisons Bureau, Federal Register, Sept 15, 2011

[73] Ibid, Mar. 13, 2013

[74] Michelle Alexander, Ibid, 133

[75] Ibid, 111

[76] "Criticizing Sentencing Rules, U.S. Judge Resigns", Special to The New York Times, Published: Sept 30, 1990

[77] "Juvenile and Criminal Justice, Luzerne Kids-for-Cash Scandal", Juvenile Law Center, updated Feb. 2012

[78] Andrew Fowler, "Exoneree Darryl Burton shares first holidays with his daughter" The St. Louis American, Dec 30, 2009 (Coverage of a 26 year old woman who spent her first Christmas with her father after 25 years in prison for a crime he did not commit)

[79] www.cca.com

[80] "John D. Ferguson, Former Commissioner of Finance and Administration For Tennessee, Named President and CEO of Prison Realty Trust, Inc. And Corrections Corporation of America", Aug 4, 2000

[81] Roger Goldman and David Gallen, *Thurgood Marshall: Justice for All,* New York, Carroll and Graf Publishers, Inc., 1992

[82] Dan Zeidman, "Senate Hearing Explores the Exorbitant Costs of Incarceration", ACLU Washington Markup, Aug 1, 2012

[83] Aviva Shen, "Private Prisons Spend $45 Million On Lobbying, Rake In $5.1 Billion For Immigrant Detention Alone" ThinkProgress.org, Aug 3, 2012

[84] Aviva Shen, "Three States Dump Major Private Prison Company In One Month" ThinkProgress.org June 21, 2013

[85] Research report of Coro Fellow, Yaa Sarpong, May, 2013

[86] Notes written by The Ethics Project's Coro Fellow, Yaa Sarpong, Aug, 2013

[87] Vicky Pelaez, "The Prison Industry in the United States: Big Business or a New Form of Slavery?" Global Research, Jan 31, 2013

[88] Vicky Pelaez, Ibid

[89] Federal Prison System, Federal Prison Industries, Inc., fy 2013 Congressional Budget, 2

[90]Federal Prison System, Federal Prison Industries, Inc., 2012, pg 1

[91] Tara Herivel, Paul Wright, *Prison Profiteers: Who Makes Money From Mass Incarceration,* New York, The New Press, 2007, 63

[92] Douglas A. Blackmon, Ibid, pgs 63-66

[93] Nate C. Hindman, " Under Fire For Dominating Small Competitors With Cheap Prison Labor" The Huffington Post Updated: Aug 15, 2012

[94] Dothan Eagle Editorial, "UNICOR Responsible For Job Loss In Alabama and Mississippi: Workplace Travesty, Sep 20, 2012

[95] Congress.gov, United States Legislative Information, H.R.2098 - Federal Prison Industries Competition in Contracting Act of 2013, 113th Congress (2013-2014)

[96] Nate C. Hindman, Ibid

[97] GEO Group, http://www.geogroup.com/history

[98] Brendan Fischer, "Violence, Abuse, and Death at For-Profit Prisons: A GEO Group Rap Sheet", The Center for Media and Democracy PR Watch, Sept 26, 2013 -

[99] Ibid

[100] http://www.sourcewatch.org/index.php/Geo_Group

[101]Brenda Fischer, Ibid

[102] James Austin, Ph.D., Garry Coventry, Ph.D, Ibid

[103] Aviva Shen, "Three States Dump Major Private Prison Company In One Month" ThinkProgress.org Jun 21, 2013

[104] Common Cause, www.CommonCause.org

[105] Intro Producer: Robert Booth. Intro Editor: Sikay Tang., The United States of Alec: A Follow-up, PBS – Bill Moyers and Company, Jun 21, 2013

[106] Ibid

[107] Ibid, www.CommonCause.org/ALEC

[108] ALEC, http://www.alec.org/membership/private-sector-membership/

[109] Douglas A. Blackmon, Ibid, 53

[110] Ibid, 66

[111] The United States Constitution, 21st Amendment Repealing the 18th Amendment to the United States Constitution, ratified Dec 5, 1933

[112] S. 714 (111th): National Criminal Justice Commission Act of 2010, introduced in the U.S. Senate, Mar, 2009

[113] David Rogers, "Republicans block justice review proposal in Senate", Politico, Oct 10, 2011

[114] "SB -1410, Smarter Sentencing Act, introduced in the U.S. Senate, July, 2013

[115] GovTrack.US, http://www.govtrack.us/congress/bills/113/s1410
[116] Naked Cowboy Rides Off With a (Partial) Win, Wall Street Journal, Jun 23, 2008
[117] Illinois v Wardlow, U.S. Supreme Court, 120 S. Ct. 673, 145 L. Ed.2d 570, Jan 12, 2000
[118] Reducing Racial Disparity in the Criminal Justice System: A Manual for Practitioners and Policymakers,
[119] Loving v. Virginia, 388 U.S. 1 (1967)
[120] Nick Dial, "Prohibitions: The War on Opium and the Chinese "Yellow Peril", featured in Law Enforcement Today, Jul 13, 2013
[121] This case was one of the first read by the author in a Southwest Reporter after graduating from law school. The exact site in unknown
[122] Deb Sopan, "Borrower Targeted for Mortgage Fraud While Bankers Got Billions, Rock Center with Brian Williams, Nov 18, 2012
[123] Ibid
[124] "14-Year-Old, Murders Her Newborn Baby", Huffington Post, Oct 4, 2012
[125] Banks Rake In $39 Billion On Overdraft Fee, by Henry Blodget, Business Insider, Aug 9, 2009
[126] War on Drugs a Trillion Dollar Failure, by Richard Branson, CNN, Dec 7, 2012
[127] Allen J. Beck, Ph.D., Paige M. Harrison, "Sexual Victimization In State And Federal Prisons Reported By Inmates, 2007", Bureau of Justice Statistics, NCJ 219414, Dec 16, 2007
[128] The Sentencing Project, "Incarcerated Women" 12, Revised, 2012
[129] President George W. Bush, 2004 State of the Union Address
[130] "Prisoner and Prisoner ReEntry", U.S. Department of Justice,
[131] Jennifer Laudano, "U.S. Prison Population Drops for Third Year as States Adopt New Policy Strategies, Public Safety Performance Project, PEW Research Institute, 202.540.6321, Aug 8, 2013
[132] Conversation with a St. Louis County Commander St. Louis County, MO, 2013
[133] U.S. Department of Justice, "Prisoners and Prison Reentry", 2008
[134] Incarcerated Parents and Their Children, Trends 1991-2007, The Sentencing Project, Feb 2009
[135] The Sentencing Project, "Incarcerated Children and Their Parents: Trends 1997-2009", 2, Feb. 2009
[136] Rethinking How to Address the Growing Female Prison Population by Julie Ajinkya, The Center for American Progress, Mar, 2008
[137] Ibid

[138] Oklahoma Lawmakers Seek to Strike Budget Balance for Prisons by Tom Lindley, modified December 9, 2010, Published: December 5, 2010, Nework

[139] Lawmakers, Fallin Approve $7.1 billion FY2014 budget, by Shawn Ashley, News Director, eCapitol, Published, Jul 2, 2013

[140] Julie Ajinkya, "Quick Fact, Women and Criminal Justice – 2009", Institute on Women and Justice, updated Sept 2009

[141] Glaze, Lauren. and Laura M. Maruschak. Parents in Prison and Their Minor Children, Bureau of Justice Statistics Special Report; Aug 2008, pg. 2

[142] Growth in Prison and Jail Populations Slowing: 16 States Report Declines in the Number of Prisoners, Bureau of Justice Statistics, Mar 31, 2009

[143] Prisoners in 2013, Advance Count by Ann Carson and Daniela Gorinelli published Jul 25, 2013, by the U.S. Bureau of Statistics

[144] U.S. Prison Population Declined for Third Consecutive Year During 2012, Bureau of Justice Statistics, July 27, 2013

[145] Chief Justice Delivers 2008 State of the Judiciary Address, February, 2008, Your Missouri Courts,

[146] Ibid

[147] Chief Justice Deliver 2010 State of the Judiciary, Chief Justice William R. Price, February, Your Missouri Courts, 2010

[148] W.W., "Prisons and crime: What's America's real crime rate?" The Economist, Feb 14th 2012

[149] Gropnik, Ibid

[150] Gerald Early, Editor, "Ain't But A Place: An Anthology of African American Writings About St. Louis, St. Louis, Missouri Historical Society Press, 383

[151] A Google search for "what does it take to raise well rounded kids, produced 24,800,000 results. Google Search, Sept., 2013

[152] Amy Capetta, "7 Ways to Raise a Well-Rounded Kid: Surround your children with love, happiness, and encouragement so they have the confidence to reach goals", Parent.com, undated

[153] Ibid

[154] Joy DeGruy, Ibid, 147

[155] from Rachel's Weekly (rachel-weekly-request@world.std.com) Peter Montague, editor

[156] See Douglas A. Blackmon, Ibid, regarding the brutal treatment of Blacks and the high rate of death following emancipation, 73

[157] Federal Register, Volume 78, Number 52, Dept. of Justice, Bureau of Prisons, Annual Determination of Average Cost of Incarceration, Federal Register Online via the Government Printing Office, FR Doc No: 2013-06139, Mar 18, 2013, 16711

[158] Tuition costs of colleges and universities; Fast Facts, National Center for Education Statistics, 2012

[159] "U.S. Falls In World Education Rankings, Rated 'Average'" Huff Education,, Sept., 2013

[160] Prison Inmates at Midyear 2007, William J. Sabol, Ph.D. and Heather Couture, Bureau of Justice Statistics, June, 2008

[161] Quoted in Shades of Freedom, 50, A. Leon Higgenbotham, Jr. 1996

[162] Reducing Racial disparity in the criminal Justice System, A Manual for Practitioners and Policymakers, 6, The Sentencing Project, 2008

[163] The Sentencing Project, http://www.sentencingproject.org/template/page.cfm?id=107

[164] Peter Montague, editor, "America's Secret War", The World Traveler, undated

[165] http://www.youtube.com/watch?v=aqitmYDsZfg, http://www.youtube.com/watch?v=kDUdniEig38

[166] Nadine Block, Spanking: Facts and Fiction , The Center for Effective Discipline, citing numerous studies, Mar, 2008

[167] Jim Burns, "Why Your Teens Need (and Want) Boundaries", Christian Boadcast Network,"

[168] Discipline, The New Bury House Diction of American English, Boston, Heinly Heinly Publishers, 1996, pg. 227

[169] Punishment. 2013. In *Merriam-Webster.com*. Retrieved September, 2013, from http://www.merriam-webster.com/dictionary/punishment

[170] Tama Lewin, "Black Students Face More Discipline, Data Suggests", New York Times, March 6, 2012

[171] Offense, The New Bury House Diction of American English, Boston, Heinly Heinly Publishers, 1996, pg. 593

[172] Marc Stroud, "Philadelphia Schools Closing While A New $400 Million Prison Is Under Construction: Could It Be Worse Than It Sounds?" June, 17, 2012

[173] "More Mentally Ill Persons Are in Jails and Prisons Than Hospitals: A Survey of the States" National Institute of Corrections, Cataloged on: Jun. 12, 2010

[174] Jeff Garrett, "After closing psychiatric hospitals, Michigan incarcerates mentally ill", Detroit Free Press, Nov. 27, 2011

[175] Ivory A. Toldson, PhD and Chance W. Lewis, PhD, "Challenging the Status Quo" Academic Success Among School-Age African American Males, Washington DC, 2012, pg. 31

[176] Ibid

[177] Executive Order -- White House Initiative on Educational Excellence for African Americans, July 26, 2013

[178] Jacqueline Rabe Thomas, "Hundreds of kindergarten students suspended from school: CT Political Mirror, May 17, 2013

[179] Colleen Curry, "Maryland First-Grader Suspended for Making Gun Gesture With Hand", ABC News, Jan. 3, 2013

[180] Laura Hibbard, "Nick Martinez, Florida Middle School Student, Suspended For Hugging Best Friend", Huffington Post Education, Nov. 4, 2011

[181] "5-year-old girl handcuffed by Florida police" WikiNews, April 24, 2005

[182] Sam Dillon, "Study Finds High Rate of Imprisonment Among Dropouts", The New York Times, Oct. 8, 2009

[183] Jeremy Travis and Sarah Lawrence "Beyond the Prison Gates: The State of Parole in America", Urban Institute, Justice Policy Center, Nov. 2002

[184] http://www.innocenceproject.org/about/

[185] Edward Lovett, "Dead Toddler Tyler Dasher's Mother Told Cops She Beat Him Because He Wouldn't Stop Crying" ABC News, Nov. 16, 2011

[186] Christ Griffin, "21 Days to Joy: A Daily Devotional to Finding Joy", St. Louis, C. Griffin Publishing, 2008

[187] The New York Times, "Action by Missouri Police Raises Questions of Racism", Nov. 24, 1991

[188] Gerald Early, Ibid, pgs 244-255 at 254

[189] Joe Nocera, "Biggest Fish Face Little Risk of Being Caught", The New York Time, Feb25, 2011

[190] Mark L. Shurtleff, quoting the majority opinion as written by U.S. Supreme Court Justice Taney in the Dred Scott Decision, *Ain't I A Man,* Orem, Valor Publishing Group, 2009, pg 484

[191] Marc Mauer and Ryan S. King, "Uneven Justice: State Rates of Incarceration By Race and Ethnicity", the Sentencing Project, July 2007

[192] Regents of the University of California v. Bakke, 438 U.S. 265, 1978

[193] Grutter v. Bollinger, 539 U.S. 306, 2003

[194] Shelby County, Alabama v Holder, Attorney General, et al, No. 12–96. June 25, 2013

[195] Richard Branson, "War on drugs a trillion-dollar failure", Special to CNN updated Dec 7, 2012

[196] Stefan B. Tahmassebi , Gun Control and Racism, George Mason University Civil Rights Law Journal Vol. 2. 1991 pg 67

[197] Kayla Webley "Why Can't You Discharge Student Loans in Bankruptcy?" Time- Business and Money, Feb. 09, 2012

[198] Azzure Gilman, "Explaining the Black-White Wage Gap", Freakanomics, Oct., 2011

[199] Marc Mauer, "The Changing Racial Dynamics of Women's Incarceration. The Sentencing Project, Feb. 2013
[200] Ibid, pg. 2

[201] Edmund F. McGarrell, Nicholas Corsaro, Chris Melde, Natalie K. Hipple, Timothy Bynum, Jennifer Cobbina, "Attempting to reduce firearms violence through a Comprehensive Anti-Gang Initiative (CAGI): An evaluation of process and impact", Journal of Criminal Justice, 2013 (Reference taken from author Chris Melde's personal copy and used by permission. For copy contact: http://www.elsevier.com/copyright Chris Melde, Stephen Gavazzi, Edmund McGarrell, and Timothy Bynum, "In the Efficacy of Targeted Gang Interventions: Can We Identify Those Most At Risk?"
[202] Marc Mauer, Ibid, pg. 3
[203] City Crime Rankings, 2010-2011, Full Rankings and Methodolgy, CQ Press, 2011
Anthony McDonald, *Risen: From the White House to Jamestown*, St. Louis, AS&J Publishing, 2010
[205] Ibid
[206] Gerald, Early, Ibid, pg 36
[207] Isabel Wilkerson, Ibid, pgs 193-194, 232
[208] Ibid, 255
[209] Gerald Early, Ibid, pg 152
[210] The Root, "Rosewood, Fla.: A Massacre That Won't Be Forgotten" 2013
[211] Ibid, "Greenwood, Okla.: The Black Wall Street" 2013
[212]Idid
[213] Seth Cagin, Philip Dray, Ibid
[214] The Sentencing Project, "Felony Disenfranchisement Laws in the United States" June, 2013
[215] Ibid
[216] Richard Fry and Paul Taylor, "A Rise in Wealth for the Wealthy; Declines for the Lower 93% An Uneven Recovery, 2009-2011", Pew Research Social and Demographic Trends, Apr 23, 2013
[217] "Civil rights advocate U.S. Rep. John Lewis urges graduates to "get in the way", Commencement Address, Union College, June 16, 2013
[218] Robert W. Peterson, "Helping Children Learn Positive Values From Sports Heroes" Scouting Magazine, January, 2001
[219] Julie West, "Children Need Clear Boundaries and Consequences", ParentingNow.org
[220] Children In Single-Parent Families By Race" National Kids Count, Apr., 2013
[221] "Why Children Need Married Parents", U.S. Conference of Catholic Bishops, 2013

[222] The Urban Strategies Council, "The Rising Costs of Incarceration: Criminal Investment Decisions" 2007
[223] Think Progress, "Ten Ways Criminal Justice is one of the great civil rights crises of our time", August 29, 2013
[224] Michelle Alexander, Ibid
[225] Lindsay M. Hayes, "Suicide Prevention in Correctional Facilities: Reflections and Next Steps", National Center on Institutions and Alternatives, Inc, 2013
[226] Common Cause web-site, http://www.commoncause.org/about
[227] Ibid
[228] Ibid

"What is past is prologue."

~ William Shakespeare

ABOUT THE AUTHOR

Christi Griffin, is a graduate of Webster College and received her Juris Doctorate from St. Louis University School of Law. She began her private law practice as a ministry in 1984 and headed one of the largest consumer bankruptcy law firms in the State of Missouri for 23 years. In 2007, Griffin began The Ethics Project to reduce wrongful prosecutions and convictions by educating the public about professional ethics. The not-for-profit organization has evolved to directly addressing the impact that crime, incarcerations and injustice have on children families and the community through education, consortiums of agencies and ministries who serve populations affected by crime, through Safe Stop & Vote for Me Campaigns, Youth Gang Summits and Empowerment Forums, Leadership Workshops, and collaborations with Ilyasah Shabazz, daughter of slain human rights leader, Malcolm X and nationally acclaimed speaker, author and CNN contributor, Victor Woods.

Griffin's service to the community includes serving as former Chair of the St. Louis Civil Rights Enforcement Commission, former member of the Boards of Directors of the Joint Boards of Health and Hospitals for the City of St. Louis, the Missouri Catholic Conference Public Policy Advisory Committee, the United Way of Metropolitan St. Louis, the Public Safety Advisory Council of St. Louis, and the St. Louis Initiative to Reduce Violence among others.

Christi Griffin is the recipient of various awards including the President's Call to Service Award and the Dr. Martin Luther King Jr. Drum Major for Justice Award. She is a Blue Ribbon Toastmaster Speaker, the mother of three adult children and the grandmother of five. She is the author of 21 Days to Joy, A Daily Devotional to Finding Joy.